SCRIPTURE UNION

BIBLE
STUDY
BOOKS

© 1971 Scripture Union
First published 1971

Scripture Union Bible Study Books
are published in the U.S.A. by
William B. Eerdmans Publishing Company.
First U.S. edition, May 1971
Printed in the United States of America.

Library of Congress Catalog Card Number: 76-151983

INTRODUCTION

This series of books forms the intensive study level of the graded, daily Bible reading plan of Scripture Union, the well-known and long established organization for the encouragement of Bible reading and study. Bible Study Books are designed to provide basic study material for the Christian who wishes to have a mature and organized guide for the whole of the Bible. The series is written by a team of evangelical scholars each of whom has earned a reputation for sound and competent biblical scholarship.

Each volume is divided into the right number of sections to make daily use possible, though dates have not been attached to the sections. Taken together the books provide a simple and complete commentary on the whole Bible.

Other series of readings are available at four main grade levels accompanied by an appropriate series of daily, expository Notes. They are used daily by nearly one and a half million people around the world and are published in 140 languages.

For further information, write Scripture Union in North America at 38 Garrett Road, Upper Darby, Pa. 19082, or at 3 Rowanwood Avenue, Toronto, Ontario.

Romans

The authorship of the Epistle to the Romans went undisputed until 1792. It can be certainly attributed to Paul. The place and date of writing can be determined with some certainty from internal evidence. Paul had not yet been to Rome (**1.**11,13,15), where a mixed church of unknown origin (Acts **28.**15) was already functioning, but he intended to pay a visit, after a forthcoming journey to Jerusalem, whither he intended to carry contributions from Macedonia and Achaia (**15.**23–32). This intention was in his mind during his residence in Corinth (Acts **19.**21). Ten years of vigorous evangelism were over, and he purposed a major new move after the visit to Jerusalem to which he looked forward with justifiable apprehension. He made this journey, and he made it from Corinth (Acts **24.**17). When he wrote to Rome, Timothy, Sosipater, Gaius and Erastus were with him (**16.**21,23). Gaius was, at least for part of his Corinthian residence, his host (1 Cor. **1.**14). Erastus was a Corinthian, perhaps a prominent figure in the city (**16.**23; 2 Tim. **4.**20), and had served Paul in Macedonia (Acts **19.**22). In Acts **20.**4 we read that Timothy, Sosipater (Sopater) and Gaius were with Paul in Corinth. Phoebe, who appears to have carried the letter to Rome, and who may have also been hostess to Paul, lived in the marine suburb of Corinth, Cenchreae (**16.**1). Set these biographical data in order, and it appears that the letter was written in the winter of A.D. 56,57. This said, the great document may be left to tell its own story, of Christian truth, and its mighty exponent.

3

Paul was no waster of words. Every ancient letter began with a note of the one who sent it, and a clear statement of the person or persons to whom it was addressed. The discovery this century of the thousands of papyrus letters, which the arid sands of Egypt have preserved, has revealed that the New Testament epistles conform to the pattern of the letters of their time. The deep matters of the faith required nothing more than the common forms of communication and the simplicities of daily intercourse in which to express themselves. They need no more today. Christ can find demonstration in our conversation, in the normal conduct of our lives and our activities. The common bush can be 'aflame with God'.

Paul passes promptly to his credentials. He is a slave of Jesus Christ, not his own, but 'bought with a price', and bound in wondrous servitude to the King of kings. It was an ancient and honourable title. Moses had carried it (Josh. 1.1 f.), and so had the prophets (Jer. 7.25). It implied a dedication to the doing of a master's will. The beautiful story of Abraham's servant on his mission to Haran is a perfect illustration (Gen. 24.1–66). And like Abraham's servant Paul was a special messenger, an 'apostle,' one sent to fulfil a particular task. The purpose and the vocation are emphasized in the closing words of the first verse. It was Paul's conviction that he was 'set apart' for the gospel of God, not merely by the formal commissioning of his fellow-Christians (Acts 13.2), but in the long-laid plan of God Himself (Gal. 1.15). In both contexts the same Greek verb is used.

Then, in swift economy of words, Paul proceeds to state the essential facts of the good news of God. He is apparently addressing in the Roman church a group of Jews and their converts. He can rely on an Old Testament background. Hence the emphasis in two verses on the Lord's earthly royalty, His power and divine Sonship, confirmed by the Holy Spirit, and sealed by the resurrection. The incarnation without the resurrection is meaningless. The two basic doctrines of the faith move together. Paul never wavered from this position. And without God revealed in Christ (John 1.18), a Christ risen from the dead, there is no Christianity.

A Meditation: 1 *Cor.* 15.12–19.

Romans 1.5–8   'All One in Christ Jesus'

Grace, the free unmerited favour of God, was the gift to all Christians. Apostleship was limited to those fitted for a special task. This clear distinction should be observed. In writing to the Corinthians Paul devotes a whole chapter to the division of labour, and variety of vocation in the Church (1 Cor. **12**). Intrusion into another's sphere of service breeds frustration and ineffectiveness, and at the same time leaves the proper task undone.

Paul's task was to summon men to 'the obedience of faith'. The genitive ('of faith') is one of definition. Obedience consists in faith (Acts **6.**7). To believe, and to commit the life to that belief, is to obey. God asks no more, no less, and in the act is involved both trust and the disciplined living which demonstrates the trust. 'The first law that ever God gave to man,' said Montaigne, 'was a law of obedience; it was a commandment pure and simple, wherein man had nothing to enquire after or dispute, for to obey is the proper office of a rational soul, acknowledging a heavenly benefactor.'

Now comes (7) the salvation, warm in its wording. 'Called to be saints' means saints in virtue of His calling. This fact is no warrant for the tactless claim to sainthood which a watching and listening world will interpret in other than Biblical terms. The coinage of speech can become debased, and the term 'saint' cannot be presumptuously used by any Christian, true though it is that God in His grace calls Christians thus.

'Grace and peace', the second the fruit in mind and heart of a proper understanding of the former, are the total of Paul's wish to the Christians of Rome. In the words are combined an echo of the common greeting of Greek to Greek, and the common (still common) greeting of Israeli to Israeli—'Shalom'—'Peace'. Paul moves into his wider sphere of witness in his very salutation.

And Jesus Christ—Jesus the Messiah—finds its fifth mention in eight verses. There is no Christianity, let the plain truth be again repeated, without the Christ of the New Testament, no deluded and defeated dreamer from Galilee, done viciously to death by collaborating priests and occupying authorities, but the Risen Son of God, from all time envisaged.

Meditation: John **1.**14–18.

Romans 1.9–12 'And so to Rome'

Paul was writing his letter to Rome, probably in Corinth, where he spent three winter months at the end of A.D. 56 and the beginning of 57 (Acts **20.**3). The Italian peninsula did not seem far away. Many years before a grand plan had taken shape in his mind, no less than a strategic attack on the Roman Empire. Cyprus had prompted the thought. He had first put it into motion when, to the annoyance of the junior member of the party, he had abandoned the sea-port, and made for Antioch of Pisidia, the bastion of Roman power in central Asia Minor (Acts **13**.13 f.).

Nine years had passed since that adventure in evangelism, and Paul had seen the fulfilment of much of that which he had set out to do. Christian churches, 'cells' of witness, were planted in the great centres of power, religion, learning and trade, in the eastern half of the Empire. He wrote from Corinth, the nodal point of central Mediterranean communications. There were Christians in Athens, intellectual hub of the world. There was an active church in Philippi, old fortress of northern Greece. Ephesus, religious centre of Asia, and proconsular seat, had its witness. Paul hoped to see the message thus placed radiate down the roads and trade-routes, permeating the vast power-system for Christ.

It was a magnificently imaginative idea. There remained the central core of the Empire, Rome itself, and the western bastion, Spain, which was to provide Rome with Emperors, as it had already provided men of accomplishment and letters—Seneca, for example, philosopher and tutor of the Emperor, and Lucan, the decade's best known poet. Spain was Paul's next objective, with Rome *en route*. Paul was not to know the painful and circuitous route by which he was to come to Rome (Rom. **15**.24–28). The pilgrimage to Jerusalem, on which he had set his heart, lay ahead, and against all opposition and advice he set out on that path—a fruitless errand, if the brief account be read aright, but one which God turned to good, for all that tumult in Jerusalem and prison in Caesarea lay in the way.

Observe in vs. 11 f. that Paul speaks humbly of gaining blessing and comfort in Rome, as well as bestowing it. Students in class, and congregations in a church, should remember that there is a two-way commerce in spiritual things, a giving as well as a getting. And could this (an awesome thought) be also true of God and us? Is this why He made us free?

Exercise: Trace the pattern of Paul's churches on a map.

Romans 1.13–17   A Gospel of which to be Proud

Paul owed, he said, a debt 'both to Greeks and barbarians'. It is curious to find the RSV persisting in this meaningless translation. Words change their meanings, expand and contract, as they pass from people to people, century to century. A 'barbarian' in the ancient Greek conception, and the language which gave it voice, was simply one who did not speak Greek. The word implied no cultural inferiority. The Greeks called the Persians and the Romans 'barbarian', while acknowledging the superiority of both, the former in material culture, the latter in political power. The 'natives' of Acts **28**.2, the 'barbarous people' of the AV (KJV), are in the Greek text *barbaroi*. Both versions miss the point. Paul simply refers to the Phoenician-speaking Maltese. In the present text the word means those who did not share completely in the Mediterranean civilization. He found such people at Lystra (Acts **14**.11). He probably met others in Illyricum (Rom. **15**.19). 'Greeks' would include Romans, for Greek was their second tongue. Paul sensed an obligation to those of his own culture and those outside it. He felt, what Jowett in his little classic called 'a passion for souls'; or as F. W. H. Myer put it in his poem on Paul:

> '*Then with a rush the intolerable craving*
> *Shivers throughout me like a trumpet call:*
> *Oh, to save some, to perish in their saving,*
> *Die for their life, be offered for them all.*'

One had already died, and in vs. 16 f. Paul speaks of the gospel which is to be the theme of his epistle. He had preached it proudly in two continents. It brought 'salvation'. In the mind's depths, for all the materialism and self-delusion which obscures reality, man is still conscious of a need for a hand reaching down. Death in this century is a less present and pressing reality than it has been in other ages. Medicine has postponed it and softened its impact. It is nevertheless true that the whole approach to life would be vitiated, and society gravely injured if all thought of another life and of ultimate justice were stamped out from the consciousness of men.

Sin still presses on mind and body for all the words used to take away its sting. Frustration and despair are still real. A sense of helplessness before forces beyond control is still a reality. Hell can be a present experience for those enslaved to evil. Christ gives purpose, 'life more abundantly', a sense of being real, clean, useful—Christ *saves*.

Thought: . . . '*The Good, the True, the Pure, the Just—Take the charm "For Ever" from them, and they crumble into dust*' (Tennyson).

Romans 1.18–21   The Reality of Natural Theology

Paul insists that, apart from the Bible and God's self-revelation in Christ, God is manifest to those with minds open to receive Him, in the works of His creation. The wonder of the world, the evidence of law, order, and purpose interwoven with all nature are evidence enough of an Intelligence behind the visible world. The first verse of John's Gospel says as much . . . 'In the beginning was a Mind which expressed itself . . .'

Furthermore, if it is clear in the world around us that Mind came before matter, it is also clear that the planning mind seen in created things also demanded obedience to certain laws. The human body can be abused, the laws of its operation disregarded, and pain follows. The land which provides our sustenance, the air we breathe, the waters upon which all life depends, are given to mankind on fixed conditions. There are laws to be observed, the selfish flouting of which, as the world is learning to its cost, brings inevitable retribution. Dust bowls, dead lakes, polluted waterways, chemical-ridden produce, smog-laden air, all carry death and pain. The planet itself could be rendered uninhabitable by its rebellious inhabitants. God put man in a garden, 'to serve it', says Gen. 2.15, literally translated, and it is part of man's reverence for his Creator to treat reverently His creation.

Paul speaks truth. Not only is the goodness of God manifest in nature, as he told the peasants of Lystra (Acts 14.15–17), but as truly, the wrath of God. So, too, in human experience. As James Froude, the historian, remarked a century ago, there is one clear lesson on which history insists, 'that the world is somehow built on moral foundations, and that, in the long run, it is well with the good, and, in the long run, it will be ill with the wicked'. Herbert Butterfield, historian of our own century, agrees. The 'wrath of God', God's inevitable reaction against rebellion and sin, is a reality, as everyone who is willing to see can see, written into life and history. Apart, therefore, from the ultimate revelation of God, which Paul was urgent to preach, man, he maintains, had the elements of truth before him. Given the desire it was possible to find God.

Romans 1.22–25   The Folly of Idolatry

We have already mentioned Paul's excursion into natural theology at Lystra. He also touched on the theme before a much more intellectual audience at Athens (Acts 17.22–31), and a remark reported by Luke from that address has significance here. God, Paul maintained to the philosophers, set man in a context of order and purpose, 'that they should seek God, in the hope that they might feel after Him and find Him' (27).

In the quest, something went awry. In arrogance and selfishness man sought a deity to tame and to serve him, instead of a Being to whom he could give himself in worship and surrender. He made God in his own image, as the psalmist chided: 'You thought that I was one like yourself' (Psa. 50.21). The beauty of Greek art could not conceal the fact that the lovely statues of Apollo, Zeus, and Athene were only Greeks as the Greeks saw themselves in their moments of self-exaltation, while the myths and legends which surrounded them told of caprice, sensuality, cruelty and pride.

Idols were the result of this perversion in man's quest for God, and they revealed the point Paul makes, man's self-willed misreading of the evidence which God had set before him. And idols were everywhere. It is difficult for a modern Christian to grasp the pervasive nature of the paganism with which his spiritual forbears had to deal. Many pages in Tertullian reveal vividly the practical difficulties which at every turn confronted the Christian in the ancient world. 'Why, even the streets and the market-places,' he writes, 'the baths and the taverns and our very dwelling-places, are not altogether free from idols. Satan and his angels have filled the whole world.' It was worse than this. The conscientious Christian had to absent himself from public festivals. They opened with pagan adoration and sacrifice to an idol. His membership of a trade guild, and in consequence his commercial standing and goodwill, involved the awkwardness of 'sitting at meat in the idol's temple'. His very shopping raised the problem of meat which had been sacrificed to idols. And still worse. Man becomes like the object of his worship, especially if it is a projection of his own evil. This is the purport of the climax in v. 25.

Meditation: We shall be like Him.

Romans 1.26–32   The Contemporary Scene

Paul was writing during the principate of the young profligate Nero when Roman society was sunk in hideous vice. It has been left to the present day to produce again on the stage the nude and open sexuality which scandalized the more sober writers of Nero's day. Petronius, so ably portrayed in Henryk Sienkiewicz' historical novel *Quo Vadis*, was writing, at about the same time as Paul, a piece of fiction which has partly survived. It concerns the base doings of three Greek scamps in the sea-ports of Campania, and is dark confirmation of all Paul here writes. Anyone who seeks evidence in support of the apostle's grim description can read Petronius' *Satiricon*, Seneca's *Letters*, Juvenal's *Satires*, Tacitus' historical works, and Suetonius' *Lives of the Caesars*. Paul was writing to dwellers in Rome, some of them 'of Caesar's household' (Phil. 4.22), who had all this before their eyes.

The close of this chapter is a warning to all peoples and all ages. To read it in our own 'permissive society' is to encounter a challenge to be strong in faith, determined in our committal to God, urgent in our evangelism. Paul is describing a society which had abandoned God. He is diagnosing the malady from which Rome was to die, for no great nation has ever yet been destroyed by a foe from without which has not already destroyed itself by corruption within. Such sin carries its own penalty, its own damnation. The time is here when Christians must show, as they were called upon to do in Rome, by word, act, and manner of life, their difference.

The last verse expresses ultimate rebellion. Sin falls under four heads. First stands fleshly sin, so obvious, so disreputable and withal, at times, so pitiable. Secondly comes spiritual sin, pride, vanity, lust for power and the legion of the like, respectable, yet treacherous, too often well concealed, and altogether damnable. Thirdly follows diabolical sin in which evil becomes an object of love for its own sake, sin's judgement on itself, the final fruit of unrepentant wickedness. Finally, comes blasphemy, that conscious hostility to God which the Bible defines in its final consummation as the 'sin unto death', and which finds no repentance because it is never committed until all desire for repentance has been wilfully rejected.

Questions for further study and discussion on Romans ch. 1

1. 'True freedom consists in service.' Apply this to the life of the Christian.
2. 'The Incarnation without the Resurrection is meaningless.' How do the Gospels illustrate this truth?
3. Study 'grace', its definition and various meanings. Consult the dictionary and Bible commentaries.
4. How are obedience and faith linked?
5. From what is the Christian 'saved'?
6. What is 'natural theology'? What does creation teach of God?
7. How does Psa. 50.21 illustrate idolatry?
8. How does 'permissiveness' in ethics and morals run counter to Christianity?
9. Why must sin, tolerated and cherished, grow more heinous and destructive?

Romans 2.1–4   'All Have Sinned'

In the next chapter Paul makes one of the great evangelical statements of Scripture: 'All have sinned and fall short of the glory of God' (3.23). Christianity maintains that at some point of time man, self-conscious and free, set his will in opposition to the will of God, and that ever since humanity has followed suit. Nor can individual man shift the burden of that responsibility on to history, heredity, environment. Professor Butterfield, the historian already quoted, says with striking simplicity: 'It happens to be a fact that I can recognize responsibility or freedom in myself—I can feel more internally sure about the fact that it was possible for me to have helped doing this or that than I can about the matters that belong to external scholarship.' No honest man will deny the personal application of that remark. We are all, in our more candid moments, conscious of the fact that we bend more easily to ill than good, that we seek with greater ease the good of self than the good of others, that our very virtues are based more on fear of punishment than on love of good, and that pride, self-assertion, arrogance, the very element and essential of all sin, mingles itself like a pervading poison with all our pretence and practice of good. In short, to apply a famous dictum, if there were no doctrine of a Fall and of Original Sin, 'it would be necessary to invent one'.

Paul finds it necessary, before proceeding to this assertion, to meet an objection. He has described in vivid terms the moral breakdown in contemporary society, but he is also conscious of a counter-argument, and pictures himself in debate with an objector. There were, firstly, good pagans. We have mentioned Seneca, destined like many Christians, to die at Nero's hands. He wrote at the same time as Paul was writing, and his attitude to moral evil was so uncompromising that Tertullian spoke of him as 'often one of us'. But Seneca, for all his goodness, illustrates Paul's point. His tutelage of the youthful Nero led him into horrifying compromises which betrayed all his aspirations, and revealed his dire need.

Secondly, came the Jew, confident in his election, certain of his righteousness, proud of the Law. Paul will soon proceed to show what the Law really signified, and the hollowness of all Jewish pride.

Romans 2.5–10   Paul and James

The last verse of yesterday's reading spoke of a tremendous responsibility. Man can presume upon the grace of God, and imagine that His love is mere indulgence. The first verse of today's reading expresses in awesome terms how heavy a load such trifling with eternal things is upon the soul of man. To treat the grace and kindness of God lightly is to encounter the inevitable severity of God's hostility to sin.

Paul proceeds to insist upon certain principles. First, God will 'render to every man according to his works' (6). This verse must be steadfastly borne in mind by those who study the great doctrine of this epistle—justification by faith. There is no contradiction between Paul and James. To Paul, it was no faith which did not issue in deeds, conduct, and character.

The next two verses open the theme of God's impartiality. There is no covenant of indulgence for those who had known God best, indeed responsibility is deepened. For Paul, a rabbi and a Pharisee, such a notion was revolutionary, and emphasizes the transformation which Christ had brought to his mind. In the strength of God's Spirit a whole way of thought, a life-long pattern of conviction, had been broken. When Peter was summoned to Cornelius' home in Caesarea, the same conviction gripped him, and filled him with wonder (Acts **10**.34 f.). And for us who read their words the wonder is that Christ could command such obedience, and induce such change. It prompts us to ask how deep the transforming influence of the indwelling Christ has penetrated into our prejudices, our modes of thinking.

The 'factious' of v. 8 are the rebellious. This is the essence of sin, for man has chosen sin in open and self-willed rebellion against God. 'One of the greatest deficiencies of our time,' remarks Professor Butterfield, 'is the failure of the imagination or the intellect to bring home to itself the portentous character of human sin.' André Gide is expressing the mind of 'factious' or 'contentious' (AV[KJV]) man, when, in *The Prodigal Son*, he extols the will to independence as the birth of human freedom and of man's responsibility for his own life. In the notion that human independence can only be secured by severance from God lies the fount of all disaster, and along that path come the fiercest of temptations.

Romans 2.11–16   God's Impartiality

Verse 11 forms a text which is expanded in the remainder of the passage. It is a theme which we could wish had been more fully developed, but Paul was content to make his main point, and that was that the mere possession of the Law conveyed no special privilege. In fact it sharpened responsibility.

In v. 13 are echoes of a rabbinical debate of the sort beloved by the scribes. Some quoted: 'If you will diligently hearken . . .' (Exod. **15**.26) as a proof that doing was less important than hearing. Paul generally was reflecting the nobler view of the school to which he belonged, the Pharisees. 'Not learning, but doing is the Leader', runs one Pharisaic commentary. The interest which emerges from thus closely marking Paul's words is his intimacy with the forms and language of current theological debate.

There is also apparent to anyone familiar with Greek thought, another clear indication of the same versatile scholar's complete

12

familiarity with Greek thought. This is a phenomenon which is notable in 1 Cor. 1—4, a passage of sustained irony which could not have been written by anyone unfamiliar with Plato and the Stoics.

Paul's knowledge of the Stoics, the noblest school of philosophy active in the world at the time, was clear in his address to the Athenian Court. It is as obvious here. The Stoics had much to say on a law naturally written in the heart, and were the first Greeks to use the term 'conscience' in Paul's sense. And it was four centuries since Aristotle had written in his *Ethics:* 'The truly educated man will behave as if he had a law within himself.' It was five centuries since Sophocles had made Antigone confront the tyrant, who demanded obedience in all he said, with the magnificent remark that 'there are unwritten and irrefragable ordinances of Heaven', which those conscious of them cannot break.

Paul was aware of such ideas and the passage is further evidence of his familiarity with the patterns of thinking in the world to which he brought the gospel. An example lies therein. Paul's famous word to the Corinthians, written six or seven years before (1 Cor. 1.18–31), implied no abandonment of all available means of communication with his contemporaries.

Romans 2.17–21   What of Example?

C. H. Dodd calls this passage 'fiercely satirical'. It is better described as ironical. Human pride, the most elusive and persistent of man's vices, can turn into a boast the very grace which should humble and the privilege which should inspire a lowly gratitude. It transforms the standing with God which the sinner has done nothing to merit or to win into a claim to excellence.

In v. 18 the grounds of the Jew's pathetic boasting was reviewed. They knew the will of God and 'approved what is excellent'. The R.S.V. translation is not good. Phillips' 'appreciate moral values', and the phrase 'aware of moral distinctions' of the NEB, are nearer to the Greek. Paul uses the words again in Phil. 1.10. Read vs. 9 f. in that chapter. The passage may be rendered: 'This is another prayer I pray, that your love may increase more and more in discernment and all manner of perception, so that you may judge what is right and wrong, and be sincere and safe from stumbling until the day of Christ. . . .'

That is, discernment and perception are needed if we are to judge right and wrong. The phrase, here and in the Philippian letter, means literally 'test out things which differ'. It is the verb of Rom. 12.2: '*prove* what is that good, acceptable and perfect will of God'

13

(AV[KJV]). It referred, in its common Greek use, to auditing and scrutinizing the accounts and conduct of office. Both AV and RSV assume that 'things which differ' are things which are better than ordinary, and this is the rendering in both passages. But 'things which differ' are surely more likely to be ethical opposites. Hence the Jew's boast. He had the Law, which prescribed for him the clean and the unclean.

It was a fact that, as no other nation, he had a notion of the holiness of God. It was true that he was, or could have been, 'a guide to the blind, a light to those who are in darkness, a corrector of the foolish, a teacher of children . . .' Such enlightenment should have made his nation that which it was from all time designed to be—a missionary people. Isaiah had glimpsed and preached that truth. It was part of the promise to Abraham (Isa. **45**.22; **52**.10; Gen. **18**.18; **22**.18; **26**.4; **28**.14). It was a privilege and a responsibility. To corrupt it into a theme for pride was heinous sin.

Romans 2.22–26   The Testimony of Israel

Among the greater characters of Israel there was always a realization that the honour of their God was in their hands. Note the significant phrase in the story of Abraham and Lot (Gen. **13**.7–9)—'the Canaanites and the Perizzites dwelt in the land'. It was this which made strife in the camp of Abraham serious. Observe, too, Ezra's remark (Ezra **8**.22). He had boasted of his God.

And now Paul in v. 24 quotes the Septuagint rendering of Isa. **52**.5. In the prophetic passage it is the degradation and misery of Israel which forms the basis for the Gentiles' scorn. What sort of God, they said, so abandons His people? This is more than once the theme of O.T. prayer.

Paul gives the words another twist. Like people, like God. If Jews have a reputation for vice, then the Gentiles' response will inevitably be that their God is base. There was some reason in the assumption. Man becomes like the object of his worship, and if man creates an object of worship out of his own mind, that deity inevitably reflects its origin, and courts rejection.

Paul is writing, no doubt with some knowledge of Roman Jewry, and there is some contemporary evidence that all was not well with the reputation of the Jews. Probably a decade later than the writing of the letter to Rome, Joachin ben Zakkai spoke with scorn of Jewish morals. The date might imply that it was a reaction to the terrible experience of the Great Rebellion (A.D. 66–70), and the destruction of the Temple, Jerusalem and Palestine. Matt. **23**, however, suggests that the roots of moral corruption went deeper in time, and found their ground in a religion turned legal, formal and unspiritual.

This was stern language. Of what use the Law if the Law was flouted by its advocates? Nor is this irrelevant to those emancipated from the Law in Christ. Christ is dishonoured if those without Him walk more righteously than those who profess His name. As John wrote many years later: 'The one who professes to abide in Him *is bound* to walk as He walked' (1 John 2.6). There is a debt of love, a binding obligation, and doctrine is tested by its fruit. So we prove the validity of religious experience. Unless that experience involves a reorientation of the will, a setting of the affections in the direction of the moral excellence revealed perfectly in the Person of the Lord, it is no true experience of God, but a sham, a futile stirring of the emotions, self-exaltation, and a pose.

Romans 2.27–29   Outward Sign or Inward Reality

'The men of Nineveh,' said Christ, 'will appear at the Judgement when the men of this generation are on trial, and ensure their condemnation, for they repented at the preaching of Jonah' (Luke 11.32, NEB). Paul is saying in the technical language of Judaism, that the Gentile, if he observes the moral law as conscience reveals it to him, wins the favour of God, but that the Jew, in spite of, indeed because of, the physical sign in his body, falls under condemnation if he fails to keep the Law which has been divinely given him.

It is a moot question how far the highly specialized language of the Judaistic debate should be kept in translation. Involved in the whole process is the other question—when translation becomes paraphrase. Other modern translations should be looked at here. RSV is conservative in its rendering. A. S. Way's little known translation concludes the passage well: '*He* is the Jew who is so in his secret soul; and his is the true circumcision—that of the heart, consisting in the Spirit's presence, not in observance of the written letter. Men may have no praise for such a man—God has'. This is paraphrase, but legitimate.

The argument appears remote from today and its ways of thinking. In the particular form in which we find it, it *is* remote. But consider two points. First, imagine its impact in the Roman Jewish community. A Jew, Paul points out, can be a transgressor of the Law, in spite of his possession of the Law, and the physical mark of the Covenant in his body. He has an outward sign which does not vary as may the condition of his heart. That sign can be a reminder,

15

a challenge, an encouragement. Hence an undoubted blessing, and an advantage. Hence, too, a responsibility.

Secondly, remote from everyday thought though this argument may be with its symbolic language and strange imagery, the principle applies to the Church. No outward formality, no ritual of worship, no religious attitudes or practice of Church observance, no form or ceremony, no membership of organization or system, no right of birth, nothing devised of man, can replace the true experience of Christ in rebirth and salvation, genuine committal to Him, and continued practice of His presence.

Romans 3.1–4   The Jew's Advantage

This passage is a brief preview of chs. 9 —11. Paul seems to pause at his last conclusion, wondering whether he has hit his fellow countrymen too hard. Some might imagine that he had concluded that the Jew had no special privilege whatsoever, and that the sign of the Covenant had no significance apart from a change in the heart.

In fact, that statement comes very near the truth. But Paul was a 'Hebrew of the Hebrews' (Phil. 3.4–6), and also remembered, perhaps, a word of Christ (John 4.22). On both counts he felt impelled to say a word of encouragement. The first question literally runs: 'What has the Jew over the rest?' It continues: 'What help is the sign in his body?'

He sums it up in v. 2. The Jews have the records of God's own self-revelation. Why then 'To begin with'? Paul has in mind the whole rabbinical argument of the three later chapters (9 —11), and the list of advantages abruptly cut short in this verse could be completed from 9.4 f. To be the guardians of God's revelation of His Person and His Plan for man was an immense privilege.

Then Paul remembers the thread of his earlier argument. The Jews had much at God's hand, but they used it ill. They were given commandments, not privileges. Special choice involves a special duty. Some, to be sure, failed to see this. They did not believe (3). Paul is treading carefully. It was a remnant only who believed, and to this fact the O.T. is witness. And now it was 'the Remnant' again, who had grasped the truth that Christ fulfilled, concluded, and gave significance to the Law.

Did the vote of 'some', even of a majority, invalidate truth? God forbid. This is the gist of Paul's argument. The verdict of the multitude is no expression of basic truth—neither in time past nor now. God works through minorities. It is a truth worth remembering when alone, or when a tiny band faces overwhelming odds. It is worth remembering in society at large. It is worth considering in the context of history, when so many seek cheap accommodation with secular thought. To belong to 'the Few' is a privilege.

Romans 3.5–8   A Theological Quibble

It has been remarked before that anyone sensitive to the ways of Greek thought recognizes in Paul's writing, in a host of subtle ways, his Greek outlook, which complements his equally obvious Jewish insights. The imaginary debate with a Jewish objector which is the key to this passage is typical of some of the writings of popular Stoicism.

The objections brought up by the supposed antagonist appear in this passage at their most obscure, but the argument Paul deals with is one which was not uncommonly advanced against his own doctrine of salvation by grace, and he was peculiarly sensitive to it.

It was simply this: if a man sins, his sin is a foil to God's righteousness, the contrast setting God's holiness in higher relief, just as darkness would not be known without light, and pleasure is made more comprehensible by pain. Therefore, the pernicious conclusion follows, if a man's sin enhances the glory of God, why should he be condemned for it?

The rift in the logic is obvious. If God could take joy in another's sin, because thereby He was exalted, it would follow that God was imperfect Himself. The whole argument is absurd, and Paul is almost apologetic in advancing it (5): 'I speak in a human way', that is: 'This is common argument.'

But although the logic seems absurd, and the very drift of the argument almost blasphemous, is not the same sin apparent in more than one sphere of modern theological thought? By one means or another, by diminishing man's responsibility or by misrepresenting God, man, the sinner, seeks to avoid the admission, in all heinousness, of his sin. The modern theologian, compromising with 'permissiveness', murmuring excuses about 'situation ethics', speculating on God's 'involvement' in the world, and avoiding the Bible's downright condemnation of sin, has no cause to be impatient with his ancient counterpart.

Questions for further study and discussion on Romans chs. 2—3.8

1. How does man 'fall short of the glory of God'?
2. How is sin related to rebellion? What is 'the Fall'?
3. 'A privilege always carries a duty or a responsibility.' How can this be illustrated from the Jews?

4. What place should ethics have in Christian preaching? Illustrate from Paul, James and Peter.
5. 'The doctrine of the Remnant.' Where does the Bible, in both Testaments, speak of this? What is its significance today?
6. 'All sin is accompanied by a faulty conception of God.' Is this true?
7. Are moral standards variable in accordance with 'the situation'?

Romans 3.9–12 All Equal in Sin

As the imaginary discussion continues, Paul returns to the equal condemnation under which both Jew and Gentile stand. Both are 'under the power of sin' (9). The RSV rightly renders it thus. The Greek phrase simply says 'under sin'. It occurs again at the end of 7.14, and in Gal. 3.22. It occurs in Eph. 1.22: 'under His feet', and in 1 Pet. 5.6. In all such contexts it implies subjection, reduction to impotence, and bondage. In both Christ's teaching and Paul's, sin is a bondage and a servitude (John 8.34). Rank and station are a mockery among slaves. Hence the equality of Jew and Gentile, sharers of a common tyranny.

Paul then proceeds to a 'catena', or 'chain' of quotations. Two or three points of interest emerge. First, note Paul's identity with the manner and form of scribal and rabbinical debate. In the interplay of theological argument during the Passion Week between the Lord and those who thought to discredit Him, O.T. texts were used in this fashion. See, for example, Matt. 22.42–44 and John 10.34–36. The latter context is striking. The Lord's use of a text, while not entirely unrelated to the original setting of the word, was considerably adapted. Adopting the rabbis' line of argument, He struck them down with an O.T. phrase.

When quoting O.T. scriptures it was not the practice to give particular attention to all aspects of the context. This is the second point to note. Paul's quotation in vs. 10–12 is from Psa. 14.1–3, where nothing attaches the words peculiarly to Jews. This, however, was not an illegitimate use of O.T. quotation. It was an accepted use of sacred texts, and must not be judged by alien standards of argument. A Jew would regard a quotation as authoritative irrespective of context. It must also be noted that Paul was himself writing what was to be Scripture. His use is sanctioned by divine authority.

The O.T. made the mental background of the Jews to whom Paul primarily wrote. Christ's conversation with Nicodemus can be properly understood only if it is realized that the learned rabbi knew by heart Ezek. 36.26—37.10. The letter to the Hebrews reveals the same intellectual background in those addressed.

For us, in the third place, there is a solemn warning not to treat the O.T. with less than the reverence it claims. We have here another illustration of how inextricably woven is the Old with the New.

Romans 3.13–18 The Old Testament Speaks

Verse 13 is an exact quotation of Psa. **5.**9, as it appears in the Greek O.T., the Septuagint. The original appears to be directed by David against the rebels in his kingdom, if Pss. **3—6** are correctly ascribed to the time of the monarch's retreat before Absalom.

Verse 14 is a freely quoted version of Psa. **10.**7, of unknown reference, while vs. 15–17 are selectively extracted from Isa. **59.**7 f. It is interesting to observe the workings of the mind of a man taught to think and express himself within the framework of O.T. language and thought. It is important always to remember, in reading Paul's letters, the Epistle to the Hebrews, Peter's five addresses in the opening chapters of the Acts, and also much of what the Lord Himself said, that the communication presupposed such habits of thought and expression, and such a frame of reference.

The purpose of this catena of O.T. quotations is to establish, by appeal to the very oracles of which the Jews were the custodians (2), the sinfulness of Jewry, and the potency of such quotation in the argument is beyond doubt. Nor must it be supposed, easily though the words of the O.T. came to his lips, that Paul's quotation was haphazard. . . .

First, he establishes by quotation the charge of universal sin (10 f.). He proceeds to reinforce it (12), and to illustrate the rebellion of the heart by the baleful utterances of the lips, words fraught with death and corruption, tongues dedicated to deceit, and malice that kills in their words (13). Their speech betrayed the noble functions of speech, calling down harm, and giving expression to the bitterness of the godless personality which sought such self-revelation (14). It is word and deed which betrays the soul's condition. Words are the revelation of thought, and that which lays hold upon the mind turns inevitably into action (15). The world's violence begins in the mind. And the evil abroad in society at large is only the collective outcome, the total individual wickedness. Ruin and misery are inevitable results (16). Peace vanishes, in the life of men and society (17), and all because men fail to 'stand in awe, and sin not' (18 and Psa. **4.**4, AV[KJV]). A devastating build-up of quotations, in fact.

Romans 3.19, 20 The Purpose of the Law

These two verses round off a section of the letter which began at **1.**18. We shall take them in turn: *Verse 19.* Paul has been quoting from the Psalms and Isaiah. His reference to 'the Law' obviously refers to these passages. It follows that he is using the term in a special sense. The Law is referred to some seventy times in the letter, and is used in four different senses (i.e. the Pentateuch, **3.**21, where it is distinguished from the prophets; a principle, **3.**27; **7.**21,23,25; **8.**2; the law of God, **2.**17 ff., 23 ff.; and in the present passage, where it obviously refers to the O.T. in its entirety). The meaning of this verse is that, if those who have God's revelation are condemned by that very revelation, how can anyone else claim righteousness?

Verse 20. Hence arises a daunting thought. Of what use is the Law? The question opens up a whole important facet of Pauline and Christian thinking. The Jew believed that he was just in God's eyes if he kept the Law. That was the position of the rich young man who came to Christ with a vital question (Luke **18.**18–27). His shallow thinking imagined that he had actually kept the Law, until Christ's probing showed how imperfect he was. The disciples' question and Christ's obscure answer were a foreshadowing of what Paul is to make clear in this epistle—the true purpose of the Law, the dilemma of conviction of sin, and God's remedy—justification by faith.

Paul had pondered long over the meaning of it all. As a Pharisee he had dedicated his life to the keeping of the Law (Phil. **3.**4–6), and yet had no peace nor satisfaction (the theme closes ch. **7**). But the Law was not without purpose, impossible though it was meticulously to keep it. In a flash of revelation Paul saw the truth. The Law revealed man to himself, showed him the righteousness of God, and how far short he fell of its demands, set before him the nature and the seriousness of sin, and therefore, by immediate implication, his dire need of a Saviour. The first necessity if a man is to come as a penitent to God must be a deep realization of his natural helplessness. This, Paul saw, was the prime function of the Law.

Romans 3.21–25a   The Universal Condemnation

The way is now clear for the great affirmation. It has been demonstrated that Jew and Gentile stand alike condemned, and that the only advantage the Jew had was the clear proof of his need by the very impact of the Law and the revelation of divine demands implicit in it. Nor, says Paul, was this alien to the O.T., in both the Pentateuch and the Prophets, had they been properly read and understood (21). This is important. Paul implies that the legalistic Judaism from which he was emancipated by his conversion, was not a true development of the O.T., but a sterile perversion of it. There was another tradition, traceable to Abraham, who later is to provide a striking illustration of the theme (ch. **4**), and also prominent in the message of the prophets, who in no way saw the Law as the final revelation of God (Isa. **1**.1–18). Paul was abundantly right. The theme of the N.T. emerges again and again in the O.T. (Psa. **51**.16 f.). Hence the heresy of Marcion in the second century, calling on the Church to abandon the O.T. Hence the need today to reaffirm the unity of the Bible. Paul was preaching no new version of God's revelation. He was calling Jewry back to their real heritage, from the blind road into which Pharisaism had led it.

God's righteousness is shown to be unattainable by the Law. To fall short of His glory is to betray the prime function of our being, to demonstrate the marring of the divine image in which we were created. Hence a clear definition of sin (23). See Psa. **4**.4 and Isa. **43**.7 for the germ of Paul's thought in his comprehensive statement.

Justification (24) is, as the Westminster Shorter Catechism puts it, 'an act of God's free grace, wherein He pardons all our sins, and accepts us as righteous in His sight'. This is through 'the redemption which is in Christ Jesus'. Redemption, in the meaning of the Greek word, is the act of buying a slave out of bondage to set him free. A ransom, in other words, is paid, just as Israel was redeemed from bondage in Egypt (Deut. **7**.8) and in Babylon (Isa. **51**.11). See also Gal. **3**.23—**4**.7. Our justification rests on the fact that God, of His own free grace, has intervened to rescue His people from bondage to sin. It follows that the redeemed are those who accept emancipation. It follows, too, that they must *believe* to do so.

Romans 3.25b–27 The Sacrifice

Verse 25 has been divided to secure a logical end to yesterday's note, and a firm beginning for today's exposition. It will be necessary, however, to go back to one term in yesterday's note. The word rendered 'expiation', the 'propitiation' of the AV (KJV), derives from a verb which most commonly means to 'expiate' a sin, that is, by some act of ritual or sacrifice, by some payment or satisfaction given, to annul the guilt incurred by the commission of a sin. In the O.T. the formalities whereby the priesthood or the people were cleansed from defilement are described as 'making propitiation' or 'atonement'.

In the present passage Christ is set forth as the means by which moral guilt may be annulled, and that is obviously an act which God alone could determine and perform. This is why the RSV avoids the term 'propitiation'. The word suggests the placating of an angry God, and although God's implacable opposition to evil in all its forms may properly be described as 'wrath', that is not the whole theological picture. Paul here means that God 'puts forward' the means whereby the guilt of sin may be removed and He does this through Christ.

It was 'by His blood' because Christ had to die to make such atonement possible, the last, complete and all-satisfying sacrifice. Again the O.T. is drawn into union with the N.T. And yet again, how could such sacrifice be effective in its operation unless those for whom it was made regarded it as such and received it? Faith is that act of receptivity and committal whereby God's means of grace is received in gratitude and appropriated into the life. Where grace meets faith, there is redemption.

We have passed through three word pictures. God justifies: He takes the part of a judge who sets the prisoner free, absolving him from guilt. God redeems: He pays the slave's ransom and liberates him. God cleanses: He takes the place of the priest who makes expiation. To those trained in the imagery of the O.T., each metaphor was vivid and complete.

Thus God can redeem without loss of righteousness (25,26), without betrayal of principle, without ceasing to be Himself. He is 'faithful and *just* to forgive us our sins' (1 John 1.9, AV[KJV]). God remains God, no whit of His holiness diminished. The judge is not unjust; the emancipator pays the full price; the expiation is complete.

Meditation: Isa. **45**.22. '*I looked until I could have looked my eyes away. There and then the cloud was gone, the darkness had rolled away and I saw the sun*' (C. H. Spurgeon).

Romans 3.28–31   A Firm Conclusion

'Therefore we conclude. . . .' (28 AV[KJV]) is a better rendering of the opening phrase than that of the RSV ('For we hold that'). The words ring with the confidence of the writer. Such firm conclusions were wrought out in anguish of soul in the years of retreat and searching which followed the shattering event of the Damascus Road. 'A man' (28) means any human being, and leads to the fuller definition of the next verse .There cannot be two distinct religious systems, one based on the Law and applicable to a Chosen People, and the other based on faith, and available for the other division of mankind, as the Jew conceived mankind. Paul is anticipating and closing a desperate breach in his line of argument which his continually present and imaginary Jewish objector might be likely to make.

And why? There were those of his race who imagined a monopoly on God. Paul's view of God was based on the old covenant, and Abraham, in this closely woven epistle, is never far from his thinking. 'In you all the families of the earth shall be blessed' implied a religion far wider than one race, and presupposed a God who was God of all men. Jew and Gentile could, by the same argument, have only one way of salvation.

Paul knew very well, from his own agonizing experience, how difficult it was for his fellow Jews to cast off the deep preoccupations of a narrow belief which had penetrated from childhood all their thinking, their whole personality, their complete view of God and God's world. He drives his argument about salvation by faith with ruthless honesty and urgency to its only possible conclusion but he passes on the same comforting thoughts which had come to his aid when he found himself thrust to his vast reappraisement of all he had believed.

Quite clearly the Lord's word, contained in the oral tradition, was in his mind. He came, He said, not to annul the Law, but to fulfil it. Hence the closing verse of this chapter, and the conclusion of a main line of the whole argument of the letter. The Law only finds meaning if it be thus bound to the ultimate revelation of God's long-standing purpose. Two further lines of proof are to follow, one in ch. 4 and another in chs. 6 to 8. The just demands of the Law, by no means made void, are met in believers only.

Questions for further study and discussion on Romans 3.9–31

1. Where, and why, does the N.T. speak of sin as servitude?
2. In modern apologetics and preaching are texts from the Bible enough?
3. What does the story of 'the rich young ruler' teach about the Law and grace?
4. How is the O.T. essential to the N.T.?
5. How does faith differ from credulity? Does doubt negative faith?
6. What is 'propitiation'? See reference books.
7. How can God be 'just' in forgiving sin?

Romans 4.1–4   Abraham, Father of the Faithful

Some reading should be done before this chapter is studied. To understand Paul's thesis we must first know about one of the great men of the O.T. Read Gen. 12—25 over the next few days and Heb. 11.8–19.

23

'By faith Abraham . . .' Four thousand years ago Ur of the Chaldees was a sea-port on the Persian Gulf, where man first learned to sail the open waters. It was the London or New York of that distant age. The dhows sailed east to the Indus valley ports, and to Ceylon, and the talk of sailors in the Euphrates valley town made one, Abraham, a citizen of Ur, aware of a great world across the waters. And down the Fertile Crescent, which made a route for the caravans up the river and round into Syria and Egypt, came the traders with stories of magnificence beside the Nile, and of the ships which came from Crete, and who told of other races, other cities, other ways. It was a varied story of human activity, with one common element for the man of Ur who listened, questioned, thought. The whole world, east, west, north, south, was lamentably lost in grotesque views of God, and soul-destroying superstition. The cruel cult of human sacrifice, the slaughter of babies, or the sacred prostitution, which he saw in Ur, were the common practices of man. Or there were worse. In Egypt they worshipped the bull, the cat, the ram, the crocodile. In Crete there were sanguinary rites of bull-fighting. . . . Abraham had become aware of nobler truth, that God was one, that God cared for man, and prompted the mind of the man who reached for Him. He had heard a voice and listened.

For thus an amazing project took shape. Abraham was the first missionary, the first man with an ardent desire to share a saving truth with his fellow men. He was aware, as perhaps no other man of his day was aware, of the vastness of the world. It was obvious that one man alone could not influence the multitude of mankind from farthest east to farthest west. But a *nation*, dedicated to the truth, might do what one man could hardly do. Hence the magnificent plan which took Abraham out from his homeland to found a nation in the clean desert—by faith. Hence the call which came, to a heart concerned and prepared to hearken. 'Abraham believed . . .'

Romans 4.5–8   Not by Works

It was a bold affirmation at the end of the last chapter when Paul claimed that the Law and the Prophets contained the root of his doctrine that salvation was by faith. It was natural enough that the great father of the Hebrew people (Matt. 3.9) should be invoked as a test case. Paul is most glad to examine the great story in that context, and does so in both this passage and the letter to the Galatians. That is why, not only the story of Abraham in Genesis, but also Gal. 3, should be read in connection with these six readings.

Paul's point has been that deeds do not win a saving merit, even if those deeds be the observance of the Law. It is rather faith, a simple trust which takes God at His word, which justifies. To the Jew of Paul's day brought up on the Law, this was revolutionary. Paul replies that, on the contrary, the most honoured figure in their history is the prime and perfect illustration.

Abraham had recognized the voice of God in the mighty conviction that held him. God was one, and God must be made known. It seemed impossible, in view of his childlessness, that he could become a great nation, that he could father the twin kindred implied in the 'stars of heaven' and the 'sand which is on the sea shore' (Gen. **22.**17). More, did not his trust endure as the years went by, and an heir seemed impossible, did he not continue to believe when it appeared that the heir, at last apparent, was to be removed from him by his own hand?

Some rabbinical thought had seen this rebuff to their legalism, and had argued that Abraham was chosen because he was the most righteous man available. There is no evidence for this. Abraham was fallible. He hastened ahead of God in the matter of Hagar. Earlier he had abandoned Palestine for Egypt. He had lied to Pharaoh.

It must have been faith which counted, as the great word to Abraham said (Gen. **15.**6). And more than a millennium later, Paul repeats, the great king and psalmist confirmed the truth. Hence Psa. **32.**1 f. which are a reaching for N.T. truth.

Romans 4.9–12 An Objection Answered

It should be understood that Paul is still imagining a debate with a keen-minded Jew such as he must often have had in the synagogues and with the rabbis (Acts **17.**2; **28.**23). The interlocutor concedes his point about Abraham. Very well, Abraham was justified by faith, but is he not the father of the Jews (John **8.**33), and does not that suggest that the dispensation of such grace is for the privileged nation only? Paul replies with a typical rabbinical argument. In writing to the Galatians he points out that the covenant with Abraham was 430 years earlier in history than the giving of the Law, and therefore took precedence over the Mosaic code (Gal. **3.**17). Similarly, here he points out that the rite of circumcision, the national 'sign in the flesh' of the Jewish people, was instituted (Gen. **17.**10 ff.) *after* the covenant, in fact fourteen years later. The argument for a Jew would be cogent. The objector is brought back to the same point of refutation in a carefully constructed argument. Verses 1–8 correspond to 3.27 f. and vs. 9–12 to 3.29–31.

Two further points might have been raised. The covenant with Abraham had international reference (Gen. **12.**3). Also this was the

25

implication of the change of name (Gen. **17.**5) from Abram, which seems to mean 'exalted father', to Abraham, which means 'father of a multitude'. That multitude, too, if the dual figure of speech is to be pressed, is of earthly and heavenly progeny (Gen. **22.**17), not only the Hebrew people who have penetrated all nations, and the Semite descendants of Ishmael, but also a spiritual posterity, those who, by faith, become the children of the father of the faithful.

It is moving to see the sweep of history which began with the obedience of one man who had a God-given vision, and pursued it in faith, one man like any other man, stumbling, rising, failing but carrying on. There is no calculating the end of one act of trust, sacrifice, and godly endeavour.

Meditation: John **11.**40

Romans 4.13–16 The Law No Negation

Paul presses his point about the Law. He insists again on the global nature of the promise to Abraham (Gen. **12.**3; **18.**18; **22.**18). If Abraham's covenanted heritage was to be confined to his own nationals, then its geographical limits were closely defined (Gen. **15.**18–21 in specific terms, and in more general terms at Gen. **13.**14 f., cf. Josh. **1.**2–4). The O.T., however, contains the hint of a wider posterity, which the N.T. takes up and claims (Heb. **11.**10; and observe Paul's point at Gal. **3.**16 and 29 where he claims Christ, and therefore Christ's people, as the true posterity of the patriarch).

This covenant, he has shown, rested on faith. If the Law, given over four centuries later (Gal. **3.**17), is to be the permanent way of salvation, a covenant is annulled twice over. First, that which was universal is peremptorily confined to one nation, and secondly and more seriously, 'faith is null and void' (14). A new principle is introduced. To inherit the promise men must keep the Law, and since to keep it is impossible, the race, which had known God's grace in the promise to Abraham, and had learned from him to move out in trust, passes under the shadow of wrath.

In v. 15, Paul digresses a little to develop this argument. He is to return to it later, and it has a place in the letter to the Galatian wanderers. He is always a little anxious lest he should appear to say that the Law was an unnecessary intrusion. The debates with the rabbis had shown him how necessary it was to make this point. The Law had its place and purpose. It did not negate the promise to Abraham. It prepared the way for the consummation of that promise, by closely defining sin. It could not cure. It could not save. Grace all along had been the way.

'Not the labours of my hands
Can fulfil Thy law's demands;
Could my zeal no respite know,
Could my tears for ever flow,
All for sin could not atone:
Thou must save, and Thou alone'

(A. M. Toplady).

Romans 4.17–21   What is Faith?

A papyrus scrap from Egypt once provided a vivid translation of
the word variously rendered 'substance' and 'assurance' in Heb.
11.1. Few have been bold enough to use the suggested translation,
but it runs: 'Now faith is the title-deeds to the things we hope for . . .'
'Faith,' said Augustine, 'is to believe, on the word of God, what we
do not see, and its reward is to see and enjoy what we believe.'
Tennyson may have had Augustine's definition in mind when he
wrote in the Prologue to *In Memoriam:*

> *'We have but faith: we cannot know;*
> *For knowledge is of things we see;*
> *And yet we trust it comes from Thee,*
> *A beam in darkness: let it grow.*

Abraham had God's word that he should have a vast posterity.
Circumstances seemed to make such an event physically impossible.
His trust was tested to the limit—and so he hoped when hope seemed
against all probability (18). He believed that at the touch of the
Creative Hand, the death which was creeping through his body
could create life. Perhaps Paul has another 'new creation' in mind,
that of which he wrote to Ephesus (Eph. **2**.1,5).
Abraham weighed all these factors. His story shows his active
consideration of such adverse circumstances. He must have been
conscious of the tug of doubt. His mistake over Hagar reveals as
much. He was tested and knew that he was being tested. But 'no
distrust made him waver . . .' (20). He conquered doubt, in other
words, for that phrase does not claim that no qualms beset his mind,
keen in its intelligence. And in the victory thus gained, he strength-
ened his faith, the aim and purpose of such testing. It 'gives glory
to God' (20) thus to trust Him, and the reward is sturdiness infused into one's faith—to the very point where faith becomes something near to knowledge, a blessed paradox (2 Tim. **1**.12). Let
Tennyson continue on that fine integration of mind and heart:

> *'Let knowledge grow from more to more,*
> *But more of reverence in us dwell;*
> *That mind and soul, according well,*
> *May make one music as before.'*

Romans 4.22–25 For Us Also

Paul sums up. James Denney may be quoted in his comment on this paragraph. He points out that it is not arbitrarily that 'faith is reckoned as righteousness'. Faith, he continues, 'is the spiritual attitude of a man who is conscious that in himself he has no strength, and no hope of a future, and who nevertheless casts himself upon, and lives by, the word of God which assures him of a future'. This is the necessarily and eternally right attitude of all souls to God. 'Now,' says Denney, 'this was the attitude of Abraham to God, and it is the attitude of all sinners who believe in God through Christ; and to him and all alike it is reckoned by God for righteousness. The gospel does not subvert the religious order under which Abraham lived; it illustrates, extends and confirms it.' (*Expositor's Greek Testament*, 2.621.)

Fittingly, the chapter ends with an affirmation of that faith in Christ which Paul was expounding (24 f.), in a rhythmical statement which may have been a credal formula for Christians, and especially Jewish Christians. It is couched in the poetic form of Hebrew parallelism, so apparent in the Psalms ('a lamp to my feet and a light to my path'). There is no theological separation between Christ's death and His resurrection, as though atonement for sin and justification for the sinner were separate divine processes. Paul always associated the death of the Lord with His rising again. He knew Christ as the Risen One who had died, and ever lived for our justification.

The RSV obscures the O.T. origins of the language in v. 25. The AV is actually closer with the rendering 'delivered for our offences.' In Isa. 53 the same verb is used twice in the Septuagint version (6,12). That chapter concludes (12): 'because of their sins he was delivered up.' This is the phrase Paul echoes, for he commonly has the Greek version of the O.T. in mind.

Let Denney conclude: 'It was the greatest display of power ever made to man when God raised Christ from the dead . . . The only right attitude of any human being in presence of this power is utter self-renunciation, utter abandonment of self to God. This is faith, and it is this which is imputed to men in all ages, and under all dispensations, for righteousness.'

A new section of the letter opens here, and runs on to **8.39**. Verses 1–11 anticipate the theme of the whole section.

Peace is the first-fruit of our justification. The rebellion is over. Reconciliation (Col. **1.20**) is won. The Christian is no longer at odds with the whole constitution of the universe. He has accepted God's will. He has set out to become the person God intended him to be. Peace is declared, and part of it is intended to be that peace of mind and heart which has ever been mankind's elusive quest (John **14.**1,27). Such is the affirmation of v. 1.

By the same blessed process God is available to us, His power ours to claim. Nothing alienates or stands between, 'so that if He were suddenly to reveal Himself we should still know exactly where we stand, and should not have to shrink away from His presence' (1 John **2.28**, Phillips). The glory of God, from which man fell disastrously short (**3.23**), is that held before us as a goal to reach for, a standing to be won by grace. Such is the hope of v. 2.

Hence victory over anything life can do. It was difficult to follow Christ in Rome. It is difficult today. No easy course is charted. There is persecution, unpopularity, loneliness. But if faith stands firm, there is the assurance that no experience is meaningless, that everything committed to God's creative hands can turn to good (**8.28**), and that the fruit of adversity is endurance. Endurance is no passive quality, no crouching under the shield as the 'slings and arrows of outrageous fortune' rain down. The shield could be a weapon of offence in the ancient armoury, and so, too, is the shield of faith. Endurance is active. It is one of the noblest of man's qualities. Such is the challenge of v. 3.

Hence character. The buffeting of the wind makes the tree strong. No sturdiness forms in the hothouse. If we would be strong we must face the storm. Christ did, and Christians are called to be like Him. Such is the prospect of v. 4.

And this is no vain hope, for God, now ours to have and to hold, fills life with His presence. His Holy Spirit indwells and sanctifies. His new-given life seeps outwards from the surrendered heart to colour thought, word and deed, and to make us like Him. Such is the consummation, the promise of v. 5.

Questions for further study and discussion on Romans chs. 4—5.5

1. What are the essential elements in 'gospel preaching'? Is there a substitute for such evangelism? Should its emphasis vary in various contexts of time and society?

2. Consider the career of Abraham in relation to faith, faithfulness, doubt, obedience and the other values and faults which Paul has mentioned.
3. What was there of similarity in Paul's and Abraham's vision of the world and its needs?
4. What is legalism? Is it found in Christian attitudes?
5. If faith and knowledge are not the same, how can Paul say: 'I know whom I have believed'?
6. What is the basis of Christian peace? By what faults or inadequacies is peace so often lost?

Romans 5.6–8 What Manner of Love?

It is after the manner of Paul to break into a lyric passage of praise. To this habit we owe some choice passages in his letters. 1 Cor. **13**, the immortal poem on Christian love, is one such flight of language. These verses are in the same style.

The love of God holds the wonder of the writers of the N.T. Look at 1 John **3**.1 and 1 Pet. **1**.3 f. And likewise these three verses. It was 'at the right time' that Christ died, no fortuitous tragedy, no chance crime, turned by the imagination of men into theological propositions. At the proper time, determined by the Providence of God, Christ died.

'The Good Man', whom the great Plato had imagined four centuries before in Athens, appeared on earth, and men did to Him as Plato had anticipated they would in a quite uncanny prophecy. 'The Good Man,' he wrote, 'will be scourged, thrown into chains . . . and after enduring every pain he will be crucified' (Plato, *Republic* 361 E). And see Psa. **22** and Isa. **53**.

In v. 7 the Greek text uses a definite article '. . . for *the* good man one will dare even to die'. It is another of those almost unconscious turns of language by which Paul demonstrates his complete familiarity with the common patterns of Greek thought. The Stoics talked of 'the Wise Man', and Greek philosophical debate was prone to such idealizations. Paul was using the language of his day. One so ideally good would be worth dying for.

But, Paul continues, it was not for such a one, but for *us*—poor specimens of the human race—that Christ chose to die. It was for 'the ungodly' (6), 'sinners' (8). Christ's death for such creatures assures us, therefore, of God's love. It went far beyond what the utmost of human love would dare to go (7). Thus, then, God reveals His love, 'presents it', as the opening verb of v. 8 literally says, in its final and unmistakable demonstration.

It is for man to choose, whether to accept or to reject, and in such choice fervently, sincerely, frankly made, lies health for the soul. The Christian does not claim perfection, but believing as he does that Christ chose to die to reveal to him the truth about his desperate evil and God's love, he personally accepts that sacrifice as his own. In this lies for him reconciliation to his God, a knowledge of forgiveness, and a spring of happiness, poise, and character.

Romans 5.9–11 Christ's Death Linked with His Resurrection

Paul is writing intensely, and on such occasions he writes in compact and heavily loaded language, difficult to translate lucidly without expansion. The AV(KJV) rendering is bold and literal, a tradition followed closely by the RSV.

It is therefore a passage in which other versions may be profitably consulted. For example, here is Phillips on v. 10: 'If, while we were His enemies, Christ reconciled us to God by *dying for us*, surely now that we are reconciled we may be perfectly certain of our salvation through His *living in us*.'

Assurance, in a word, comes from acceptance of the fact of Christ's atoning death as the basis of our salvation, and the consciousness of union with an indwelling *risen* Christ as a continuing experience.

The argument runs thus, step by step: The initial problem is the greatest. How can sinful man be reconciled to a righteous God? How can a holy God demonstrate His love for the rebel, and bestow divine righteousness on him? How that major difficulty can be overcome has been explained in 3.21–30. God has 'put forward' Christ to be an 'expiation' for our sins. His death was the demonstration, and by faith in Christ crucified, man is brought near to God.

If such grace was shown us, then, while we were yet sinners, much more, with that transaction done, can we trust the living Christ to preserve us, not only from the temptations which beset the path, but from final judgement. He died on the cross, but He rose from the dead. He lives while we live, in us, available, implicated, involved, and He will be present at the awesome encounter in another life when we meet God.

This is a thought to which Paul will return, for example in the triumphant words of ch 8. And note how intimately Christ's death is linked with His resurrection. Without a living Christ there can be no assurance, just as without the dying Christ there could be no salvation.

Verse 11 speaks of 'boasting' in God ('rejoice', RSV). Such boasting is not 'excluded' (cf. 3.27). 'To make one's boast in God is the perfection of religion' (James Denney). See Pss. 34.2; 44.8; 2 Cor. 11.17.

Pause now, as Paul does, to take stock. The relation of Christ to the race of man has been expounded in the tract of argument from 3.21 to 5.11. The first eleven verses of this chapter sum up the whole of this passage, and v. 11 is a summary of the rest. 'Therefore' can refer to the larger passage, or to either of the summaries. Paul might have ended v. 14 with a sharper reference to v. 12, and said: 'so also by one Man righteousness entered into the world, and life by righteousness'. This is what he virtually says. He is contrasting Adam and Christ. In the former the race finds a unity in the flesh, and in the sin and death to which sin is heir. In Christ the race could find unity again, a unity in the spirit, and in righteousness and life to which the spirit by faith can be the heir (1 Cor. **15**.21 f., 45–49).

The argument is theologically less potent in modern thought than in ancient and Jewish thought. The involvement of group and family in the sin of the individual was demonstrated grimly in the tale of Achan. On the other hand there is truth which might even find genetical confirmation in the argument. As Macbeth realized too late, we cannot 'with the deed trammel up the consequences'. Adam admitted a force of death into the world of men. The fatal principle gained entry into the world, and it was impossible to exclude it save by an extraordinary act. The communicability of sin, in man's close-knit society, is demonstrable. Hear Professor Butterfield again: 'If there were no more wilfulness throughout the whole of human nature than exists in this room at the present moment, it would be sufficient to tie events into knots and to produce those deadlocks which all of us know in our little world, while on the scale of the nation-state it would be enough, with its complexities, ramifications and congealings, to bring about the greatest war in history' (*Christianity and History*, pp. 37,38.)

As John Dunne said, three and a half centuries ago, 'no man is an island, entire of himself'. And have we any need to prove or to demonstrate the indissoluble link between sin and death?

Note: F. F. Bruce, in Tyndale N.T. Commentaries, *Romans*, pp. 125–131, writes lucidly on this passage.

Thought: How much do we contribute this day to the world's total of good or evil?

Romans 5.15–17   Man's Restoration

How is the image of God, in which man was originally created, restored? The Christian answer, as we have already seen, runs thus:

Man stands under condemnation, and there must be no baulking that fact in fruitless tribute to human pride. Man, too, is conscious of moral freedom, and unless the universe is a vast and incredible mockery, he *is* free and responsible. The will of God has been revealed to men, and there is not one who has wholly made that will his own. Man stands condemned. He stands condemned before God, and to deny the fact makes chaos of God's righteousness.

Nor, the doctrine continues, is divine holiness an obscure conception to be brushed aside in the name of grace. God's condemnation of sin, His wrath repelling sin and abiding upon it, are not the notions of ignorance, fear and primitive demonologies. They accompany the loftiest views of the deity, justice and righteousness. They stand or fall with the Christian conception of sin and command no less an authority than Christ Himself. They are implicit in the whole N.T., whose writers one and all insist that God's condemnation of His creatures is a serious thing dealt with in bitter seriousness by Christ.

Christianity says quite simply that God's condemnation for sinful man is removed 'in Christ'. How? The modern mind, anxious for formulae, empirical proof, and illustrative analogy, is not content with mere dogma. How can the death of 'one Christus, who was put to death in the principate of Tiberius, by the procurator Pontius Pilate', alter man's relationship to God in the twentieth century? Some, confronted with the dilemma, would answer merely with the determination of Galileo, 'Nevertheless, it does.' And, in fact, it is common human experience that the gospel works. From Paul on the Damascus Road to Augustine in the Gardens of Milan, to Bunyan, Newton, Moody and Spurgeon, dramatic conversion and the revolution of human character have been a commonplace of man's experience. To analyse the phenomenon of conversion, to unravel, as investigation well may, the psychological processes involved, neither explains the fact away nor invalidates its theology. In all history, only the Christian gospel, with its doctrine of redemption, has effected constant, widespread, and far-reaching changes in human lives.

It is demonstrable in a myriad case-histories that Christ has redeemed from fear of death and the dread of God those who in simple faith have accepted His work as being personally significant; that the power of such faith has been a deep fountain of social good and untold personal happiness; that the very image of God has been seen in clear and unmistakable lineaments in a multitude of all degrees, of all nations, who have accepted the forgiveness which the Christian gospel offers in Christ and His 'finished work'.

Note: V. 15: 'Many' is literally 'the many' (see also v. 19, where it is so translated by the NEB). This is a Hebrew idiom indicating the mass of mankind.

Romans 5.18–21   The Blessed Contrast

The conclusion, then, is: 'As through one offence the result for all men was condemnation, so also through one righteous act the result for all men is justification and life.' The comparison or contrast between Christ and Adam is thus closed, but into the situation intruded the Law (20). Sin, Paul means, preceded the Law. The condemnation which fell on sin was earlier than the Mosaic Code. The Law came to sharpen the realization of sin. See Gal. 3.19 ff. and the expansion of this concept in 7.7 ff. of this epistle. The Law made the realization of need, along with the conviction of sin, sharper, but it followed that grace was simultaneously more vividly apprehended as God's embracing and sufficient answer and remedy. Paul's own sense of triumph and gratitude rises to its climax as the chapter ends, and the close is almost a doxology.

The skill with which Paul puts the Law in its proper place should be noted. He has not lost sight of his Jewish audience, nor of the imaginary objector, who will appear again in the opening verses of the next chapter. He will not discuss the Law summarily. Nor is it his place to deal with it as sovereignly as Christ did. He merely concentrates on showing, both in the context of Adam and of Abraham, that before, and without the Law, the elements of the situation and the essentials of the problem were the same. Paul was deeply concerned with history.

He uses a vivid word in v. 20 which literally might run: 'the Law came sideways in . . .', interrupting, but interrupting with salutary purpose, a moving flow of history. Phillips is hardly correct in rendering 'the Law keeps slipping into the picture to point the vast extent of sin', for the tense is aorist. The reference can only be to the historic giving of the Law. Once it was given, sin was apparent, no longer latent, but defined, diagnosed and 'multiplied'. Grace became a dire necessity, a clamant need. Hence the vital linking of the Testaments.

Note: V. 18: '. . . condemnation for all men . . . life for all men . . .' Dr. Leslie C. Allen (*A N.T. Commentary*, Pickering and Inglis) comments that the *scope* of 'one man's trespass' and 'one man's act of righteousness' was and is 'all men'. He continues: 'The limiting phrase in v. 17 suggests that in the second case it is restricted to those who actually accept God's offer of salvation. To suppose that Paul taught the universal salvation of all individuals is to ignore the realism which years of missionary experience must have inculcated in him. "All in Adam", "All in Christ" is meant.'

Meditation: 'The last words of Mr. Honest were, **Grace reigns.** *So he left the world'* (Bunyan).

'*Could my zeal no respite know . . .*'

Romans 6.1–4 The New Life

Singlemindedly Paul has pursued his argument of sin and grace. The sharper the conviction of sin, the deeper the realization of grace, has been his argument. And now the imagined objector steps in subtly or perversely. 'If that is so, the more we sin, the greater the grace bestowed in forgiveness.' A temptation for the theologian is the verbal quibble. Exploring the infinite with finite words, forgetting the living, present reality of God in formulating propositions about Him, men have been reduced to strange dilemmas.

Paul knew that he would face such quibbles in Rome. He had, no doubt, already met them elsewhere. Hence this passage, the swift refutation, and the great statement about union with a living Christ. Baptism is presented as a symbol of death and burial. In the catacombs both fonts and baptistries are to be found, and the mode of baptism would appear to have been dictated by the amount of water available.

On the other hand, the Jew knew only baptism by immersion. Such was John's baptism in Jordan. At Masada a baptistry has been recently discovered, and, to the gratification of orthodox Jewry, the rock-hewn tank holds precisely the amount defined by rabbinical regulations as enough completely to cover a man. Such was the baptism a Gentile convert to Judaism knew. This is the background of Paul's use of the figure and the ritual for the Christian's 'burial with Christ', and his resurrection to a new mode of life.

Let Handley Moule conclude: 'The previous argument has made us conscious that Justification, while a definite transaction in law, is not a mere transaction; it lives and glows with the truth of connection with a Person. That Person is the Bearer for us of all Merit. But He is also and equally the Bearer for us of new Life, in which the sharers of His Merit share, for they are in Him. So that, while the Way of Justification can be isolated for study, as it has been in this Epistle, the justified man cannot be isolated from Christ, who is his life. And thus he can never *ultimately* be considered apart from his possession in Christ of a new possibility, a new power, a new and glorious call to living holiness.' (*Expositor's Bible*, 5.556.)

Meditation: '. . . so we too might rise to life on a new plane altogether' (v. 4, Phillips).

35

Questions for further study and discussion on Romans chs. 5.6—6.4

1. Can any form of Christianity exist without firm faith in the historic fact of Christ's resurrection?
2. What is meant by the phrase 'the second Adam'?
3. What is 'God's wrath'? How does human anger differ? Is there such a quality as 'righteous indignation'?
4. List three hymns which best express God's grace revealed in Christ.
5. What does Paul mean by the phrase 'a new creation' (2 Cor. 5.17), and John by 'you must be born anew' (John 3.7)?
6. Define 'eternal life'.

Romans 6.5–10   Risen with Christ

Union with Christ at one point, in His death, means union with Him in the whole sequence of events which followed—His resurrection and His exaltation. Victorious living, our very immortality, is implicit in this reality. To imagine that a sinner could accept the gift of grace, and then continue living his old life, would betray an error of so fundamental a nature as to call into doubt his whole affirmation of acceptance.

He who has 'died with Christ' is emancipated from a servitude (6); but is released, as death in all cases releases, from all bonds and obligations (7). The NEB is particularly good on this challenging and important passage. 'The man we once were has been crucified with Christ, for the destruction of the sinful self' (6). The new life in Christ will be the same life which Christ Himself lives, a life inaccessible to death. Something between thirty and forty years were to pass before John closed the canon of the N.T. with his Gospel and the first of his three letters which accompanied it. Over that period Paul's doctrine of union with Christ, which appears in more than one form and context in his writings, had been taught and experienced in the Church. Perhaps that is one reason why John so stresses 'eternal life' in his writings. 'Eternal life' is the life of this passage, that mode of living which Christ, risen from the dead, experiences, and which is shared by those 'in Him'.

The new life in Christ gripped the imagination of the early Church, and one of the commonest *graffiti* in the catacombs beneath Rome, so haunted by the early Christians of the city to which Paul addressed his words, is the phrase 'in Christ', scratched on wall and sepulchre in Latin and in Greek. 'Abide in Me', said the Lord in the last hours before His death, and that last talk with His disciples should be studied alongside the passage before us. Abiding is 'that continuous act whereby we lay aside all that which we might derive from ourselves, to draw all from Christ by faith' (Godet—adapted).

On that word we can conclude this note, for it provides a commencement for the next. Inevitably Paul's theme has returned to its major note. It is all 'by faith'.

Meditation: John **3**.16.

Romans 6.11–13   The Psychology of Faith

The new life in Christ is real, but must be realized. Look at each verse in turn: (*i*) *Verse 11*: 'Reckon yourselves . . .' 'Consider yourselves . . .' 'Regard yourselves . . .' The various versions strive with equal success to render a Greek present imperative. That tense implies a process, a continuing action, a repeated endeavour and obedience. The whole psychology of victorious living, of vital Christian faith, is here. We must lay hold of our potential, 'work at our salvation'. A Christian, conscious of a thrust of evil in the heart, a tug of carnal temptation, the drag and pull of old unregenerate ways of thought, speech and action, must respond by the declaration: 'In Christ I am dead to this.' So, too, seeing that the life in Christ is not repression but sublimation, when an urge to good, a movement of God's indwelling Spirit prompts to righteous action, to Christlikeness, to creative living, he must similarly respond with the declaration: 'So be it, Lord. Let me so live, so speak, so think.' The result is growth in grace, the replacement of old ways, responses, reactions, by new, godly and salutary things.

(*ii*) *Verse 12*: For, in truth, a tyranny is broken. The verse may be rendered: 'For never let sin reign as king in this mortal frame, so that you should obey sin in all its urges.' The one-time slave and subject has been liberated. He has a new Lord, and should serve Him, not the old, discredited, defeated despot. Let there be, to borrow Kipling's conclusion to *The Dawn Wind*, 'the noise of fetters breaking', when 'everyone smiles at his neighbour and tells him his soul is his own'.

(*iii*) *Verse 13*: Our bodies, in truth, are now God's temple (2 Cor. **6**.16), not mere tools and weapons (the Greek word means both) of a ruthless overlord, who cares nothing for the victims of his tyranny. We become persons in Christ, real, alive, vital, not the unloved and unregarded instruments of evil.

It is a magnificent passage. It is by faith that the Christian lays hold of his privilege. It is defect of faith that leaves him serving still a tyranny that is broken. Christ died that we might be free. He lives to keep us free.

Meditation: ... '*Bringing all my burdens,*
                 Sorrow, sin and care,
                 At Thy feet I lay them
                 AND I LEAVE THEM THERE.'

Romans 6.14–18   The New Allegiance

The passage reiterates with new urgency what has just been said. 'It is not restraint, but inspiration, which liberates from sin; not Mount Sinai but Mount Calvary which makes saints' (James Denney). Paul is going to expand this thought in the next two chapters but at this point the old difficulty of 3.8 and 6.1 comes to his mind again. It must have been a favourite objection in the hands of legalistic Jews. Hence this final refutation:

(*i*) *Verse 14* sums up, using again the imagery of v. 12, 'For sin shall not be your overlord. For you are under grace not under law.'

(*ii*) *Verse 15.* Are we then to sin because we are no longer ruled by regulations, but are bound instead by our debt of love to a pardoning and redeeming God? Banish the very thought.

(*iii*) *Verse 16.* Is it not simple and obvious truth, set in an immortal context of words by the Lord Himself, that no man can serve two masters (Matt. 6.24)? A slave, in ancient law, was the exclusive property of one master, and his one essential function was simple obedience. There are two masters for man—sin or Christ. Man is able to choose. One servitude is a heavy burden and its end is death. The other's yoke is easy (Matt. 11.30), and its end is life and righteousness. The Greek word translated 'either' is an emotive form common enough in Plato, but found only here in the N.T. It is as though Paul says: '*of course* there can only be the *two* alternatives'.

(*iv*) *Verses 17 f.* Now follows a turn of style which is often characteristic of Paul. It is part of the warmth of his character, and to be observed in such passages as Phil. 2.1–18. Paul makes some statement of profound theological truth, as he does here, and ends with the hearty assurance that those whom he addresses know the truth of it all in personal experience, and have chosen obedience and Christ. See also the severe words of 1 Cor. 6.9 f. followed by the warm confidence of v. 11.

The practical challenge which emerges is that both God and sin need servants and tools. God works through men, and sin curses the world through those in whom it dwells.

Thought: '*Christ has no hands but our hands*
            To do His work today.
         He has no feet but our feet
            To lead men in His way . . .'

Of course, says Paul half apologetically, in face of the implied thought that Christian living itself is a species of slavery, 'I am simply using a human figure of speech to get my meaning across to you' (19). In fact, trained as he was in Greek rhetoric, he had been carried on by the neat contrast he was developing between the two masters, and the two allegiances. He returns to the point to forestall an objection. Christianity is true freedom, not slavery. (See 3.5 and Gal. 3.15 for other examples of Paul's apology for such a point of style. He was too good a scholar to treat an illustration of truth, or an illuminating analogy, as if it was an expression of truth itself. Preachers and expositors should note.)

Led on by his careful parallelism, a habit of Hebrew poetry, as well as a mode of Greek rhetoric, Paul proceeds to develop the thought that in all states of life there is a bondage and a liberty. Bound like slaves 'to uncleanness and lawlessness', the pagan was at liberty in relation to righteousness. That is, as Phillips rightly renders, he 'owed no duty to righteousness' (20).

What advantage lay in such a damning freedom? None, but only horrifying recompense. With a sharp contrast between 'then' (21) and 'now' (22), Paul appeals to the fruits, the results of the contrasted attitudes. Shame and death lay on the one side. Sanctification and life lay on the other. Man is quite free to choose.

'Sanctification' merits deeper study than one brief note can give it. Paul, in fact, is returning to the thought which appeared at the opening of the chapter—'reckoning oneself dead to sin and alive to righteousness'. It is the blessed process whereby the indwelling Christ takes over a life, filling, purifying and transforming it into His own likeness. There is battle enough, as Paul is to show in the closing verses of the next chapter, but the movement is begun as soon as a sinner in faith repudiates sin's tyranny, and accepts the lordship of Christ. Such is the 'free gift'—no 'wage' but a gracious donative (23).

Meditation: '*O Christ, Thou art within me like a sea,*
Filling me as a slowly rising tide.
No rock or stone or sandbar may abide
Safe from Thy coming and undrowned in Thee'
(E. L. Pierce).

Note: Professor G. Walters has an excellent article on Sanctification in the *New Bible Dictionary* (IVP).

The subject of the previous chapter is continued, under a new figure and illustration. In the earlier passage the bondage was that of sin. Here the bondage is that of the Law. Very boldly, in view of the fact that he is addressing the Jews who must have formed a large element in the Roman Christian congregation, Paul stresses the nature and limitations of the Law.

He points out that law of any sort is master of a person only during life. Death voids all contracts. A woman, bound by the legal contract of the marriage bond, is free to marry if that bond and contract are broken by her husband's death. The illustration is only a rough analogy, for in its application it is the bonded person who himself 'dies to the Law' in sharing mystically the death of Christ. It is a difficult passage, and it is easy to appreciate C. H. Dodd's suggestion that one should not here press too far the form of the words or the elegance of the logic. One should cut right through to the question of what Paul meant. And that seems abundantly clear. As the Christian must reckon himself dead to sin and alive to the righteousness which is his in Christ, so similarly he should consider himself emancipated from the Law by a species of death, the death he shares with Christ, just as in Christ he shares Christ's new life—and death annuls all legal obligation.

To the Gentile and to the modern Christian the argument seems unnecessarily elaborate. To the Jew it was vital. The Law, since the Captivity, had meant everything. It had been the cement of their nation. And it had bulked largely in the experience of the last two centuries, during which, growing beyond its salutary function as conservator of Jewry and Judaism, it had overwhelmed all Jewish life. Paul knew the strength of the Law in personal experience. He also knew its power to daunt and to condemn. Of that he is presently to speak in terms of theology and personal experience. He had known also a vast emancipation, and is urgent to share the liberty he had found with all who would listen to him. The Galatian church had demonstrated how difficult it was for Christians, who had truly believed in Christ, to cast off the tyranny of the outmoded Law. The Epistle to the Hebrews touched the same theme.

Meditation: Phil. 3.4–10.

Romans 7.5–10   The Purpose of the Law

Paul was vividly aware that this line of argument contained a peril. He was a 'Hebrew of the Hebrews', as he told the Philippians, and he was not ready to deny the whole heritage of his race. Moreover, the O.T., the authority of which he would not have questioned for a moment, represented the Law as a gift of God, as a part of a Covenant. And he had the authority of the Lord Himself for such an attitude. The Sermon on the Mount goes beyond the Law, and the Lord in Matt. 23, in His denunciation of Pharisaic legalism, speaks with scorn of man's elaboration of the divine code, but neither in the Sermon on the Mount, nor in any contest with the scribes, did Christ sweep the Law aside as irrelevant, faulty, man-made, or contemptible.

It was essential that Paul should integrate the Testaments, that he should assert the Christian's freedom in Christ and yet show a true and salutary function for the Law. It was a brilliant stroke of theological insight to effect this synthesis, and, for the evangelism he had before him, it was a first essential. It was to be Paul's greatest contribution to Biblical theology.

What then was the function of the Law? It defined sin. The very prohibition revealed the nature of sin. An appalling phenomenon of the present 'age of affluence' is the 'permissive society' lauded by some politicians, and 'the situation ethics' of certain 'new theologians'. It is a condition marked by the discrediting, abandonment and denigration of absolute standards, and the result is a wide failure to apprehend, to appreciate and to feel the gravity of sin. There must be Law. Without absolute demands there can be no definition of sin, no challenge to it. In this sense, as Paul says, the Law brought sin into being. It located and named it.

But Law can do no more. It can convict and condemn. It cannot save. It can quicken conscience, but cannot assuage its pangs. It is only the trusted servant, as Paul told the Galatians, who cannot educate the child but can bring him to the one who can. The Law is divinely given, essential—but halts short and provokes despair, unless it be fulfilled in Christ, unless it hand over its slain victim to His resurrecting strength.

For Reference: Acts **15.**10; *Gal.* **2.**16–21; **3.**21–29; **5.**1; *Heb.* **10.**16–20.

Romans 7.11–14 The Law is Good

The Law was a way of life. Could a man but keep it absolutely he might need no Saviour. It was the spiritual tragedy of the rich young man who came to Christ that he thought that he had actually kept the Law (Mark **10.**17–22). And yet that same enquirer was troubled in heart and felt that he lacked the 'eternal life' which is the gift of God's grace. Paul knew that fact in sharp realization.

The Law was that which exposed him to condemnation, and spelt out the sentence of death.

In v. 11 there is an acute piece of psychological insight which adds a facet of truth to this fact. Such is man's fallen nature that the very definition of sin prompts to sin. The Law, says Paul, deceived me. Gen. **3**.13 provides an illustration. The prohibition becomes a challenge, provokes rebellion, suggests defiance. And always, as in Eden, there is the lurking thought of possible impunity. The Tempter turned the prohibition, intended only for Adam's good, into a force for destruction, mingling it with a lie.

It is the eternal nature of sin that it takes that which is good and transforms it into evil. Test that thought in all areas of human folly and wrongdoing and it will be seen to be true. The Law was good, but it was made by sin into a bridgehead of evil. But this raises the problem of v. 7 in a new form. Paul repels the thought that a good thing was made a source of death for him. It was part of God's intention that sin might appear sin, shown forth in its true nature, for if sin turns a good gift into a curse, could anything more sharply awaken a desire for deliverance?

To the close of v. 11 we seem to hear Paul's own testimony of his confrontation with the Law. He seems to be telling us how, in his early maturity, he had ridden smoothly along the stream of moral rectitude and reputation for piety, until he had struck the rock of the commandment: 'You shall not covet', with its implication of selfish ambition, and arrogant desire. Then, as though from an ambush, sin arose (7) and made the strong and self-reliant man aware of the ramifications of his weakness and sin (8). He discovered the Law, and with it death (9). He was struck down on the road of life (11), convicted of sin by that which he had professed with pride to follow and observe, and conscious of his desperate need. The passion of Paul's first persecution of the Christians found its deep psychological roots here. He was a desperate man battling against the urgent pressure of the devastating truth.

Romans 7.15–20   The Conflict Within

This passage has occasioned much unnecessary difficulty. To be sure, it does look like a confession of defeat, but it requires an extraordinary Christian to disclaim acquaintance with the inner strife which Paul confesses. This must be an utterance of his Christian experience, no mere recollection of unregenerate days. It requires a true Christian to acclaim the excellence of God's demands, and strive to make them real in life's experience. It is God's prompting in the heart which fires this deep desire for holiness, and this profound dissatisfaction with all achievement. It is absurd mechanically to interpret the moving words of a great and noble soul, to note that no specific reference is made in them to the Holy Spirit, and therefore to assign the confession to a section of life unblessed by the Divine Presence. It is the Holy Spirit which prompts the mood described, and the Holy Spirit which sanctions the very confession.

Paul discovered that life was a battle, and that the nature of man slips easily towards evil. Those who teach otherwise deceive those they teach. The N.T. sets no limits to our victory over sin and our baser self, but it can lead to nothing but frustration, disappointment and despair to suggest to those who accept Christ, that sinless perfection lies within easy reach and to give the impression that flawless virtue is the immediate mark and ready attainment of those who follow Him.

Two passages then for meditation: (i) 'The picture is true for the whole course of Christian life here on earth, for there is never an hour of that life when the man who "says he has no sin" does not "deceive himself" (1 John 1.8). And if that sin be but simple defect, a "falling short of the glory of God", if it be only that mysterious tendency which, felt or not, hourly needs a divine counteraction, still, that man "has sin", and must long for a final emancipation' (Handley Moule on this passage). (ii) It was said of Brother Lawrence 'that when he had failed in his duty, he only confessed his fault, saying to God: "I shall never do otherwise if You leave me to myself. It is You who must hinder my falling and mend what is amiss." After that he gave himself no more uneasiness about it.'

Questions for further study and discussion on Romans chs. 6.5—7.20

1. 'Temptation is not sin.' What does this mean? Is it so?
2. What is 'Christ's yoke'?
3. 'Christianity is a process, not a sudden attainment.' What are the implications of this statement?
4. Study 'sanctification'—its theology and its application to ordinary living.
5. Illustrate the Lord's attitude to the Law from the First Gospel.
6. 'Sin can usually be shown to be a perversion of something intended to be good.' Can you agree with this and illustrate it?
7. What is implied by the fact that the N.T. likens Christian living to the task of the soldier, the athlete, the wrestler, the charioteer, the fisherman, the farmer and the shepherd?

Bishop Handley Moule has written with deep understanding of this
passage (*Expositor's Bible*, 5.563–567). All great literature renders
up its meaning only to those who give mind and heart to the reading
of it. The good bishop gave both, and has written penetrating words
on Paul's confession. He points out that into its words 'there creeps
no lying thought "that he is delivered to do these abominations"
(Jer. 7.10); that it is fate; that he cannot help it. Nor is the miserable
dream present here that evil is but a phase of good. . . . It is a groan
of shame and pain from a man who could not be thus tortured if
he were not born again. Yet it is also an avowal—as if to assure
himself that deliverance is intended and is at hand—that the tyrant
is an alien to him as he is a man regenerate . . .'

The exclamation of thanksgiving in v. 25 shows that the deliverance he longs for is no postponed and promised consummation,
to be granted only in another life. It is part of present experience.
The military metaphors of v. 23 show that the battle is on, and no
battle is static. All conflict moves towards victory or defeat. The
Christian, as Bunyan points out in his great allegory, is at war,
but need have no doubt concerning the outcome. He is certain to
win. The day will bring its test of strength and will, its wounds and
toil, but each day should bring victory closer. Our Ally is at hand,
involved in the conflict . . .

We should be grateful to Paul for this confession. It is too commonly our experience for us not to recognize in it the fight we daily
fight. This epistle is no mere textbook of theology. It is, like the
Psalms, a record of the soul. Dr. Alexander Whyte, quoted by F. F.
Bruce (*Romans*, Tyndale N.T. Commentaries, p. 151), was right
when he said that the recognition of the personal involvement of
Paul in what he wrote was a touchstone of understanding for this
epistle. Whyte said: 'As often as my attentive bookseller sends me
on approval a new commentary on Romans, I immediately turn to
the seventh chapter. And if the commentator sets up a man of straw
in the seventh chapter, I immediately shut the book. I at once send
the book back and say "No, thank you. That is not the man for
my hard-earned money".'

Romans 8.1–4   No Condemnation

The chapter falls into three divisions, of which the first, which speaks
of the Spirit as the principle of righteousness and life, covers the
first eleven verses. The opening verses are one of the great triumphant
passages to which Paul sometimes rises.

The negative in v. 1 is emphatic. 'There is therefore now no condemnation *at all* for those who are in Christ Jesus . . .' The Holy Spirit pervades the chapter. To be 'in Christ Jesus' means to be indwelt by God, to have God's power available to the outreach of faith, to be emancipated, and under no bond of broken servitude.

To 'walk . . . according to the flesh' means to live the life of the pagan world, to be the puppet and plaything of undisciplined lusts, and to know the frustrated helplessness and pain of those who know that the fruit of such living is unhappiness and defeat, but who see no hope of deliverance. The 'works of the flesh' are listed in Gal. 5.19–21. They are the base reactions to which human nature turns.

The word 'Spirit', the antithesis of 'flesh', occurs a score of times in this single chapter. To 'walk . . . according to the Spirit' is to catch the vision of God's emancipating power (2), made real and visible in Jesus Christ, God's demonstration of Himself to men (3). Christ gave the race a fresh start. In Adam all sinned. This was the contention that initiated this train of reasoning three chapters back. Christ broke the spell. Like a new Creation, a second Adam, He faced the same conditions, confronted the same temptations, but rendered up to God a perfect obedience. And so a man could be made free of Adam's corrupted race, and made one with Christ, in whom doom and defeat fell on sin. He was given a new start, the past cancelled, its servitude broken. It remained only to realize that life, and lay hold of the privilege. This is what Paul means by 'liberty' (2 Cor. 3.17; Gal. 5.13).

Meditation: The fulfilment of prophecy in Paul's doctrine. See Ezek. 36.25—37.14 and Jer. 31.33 f. (The Lord was referring to both passages in His conversation with Nicodemus—John 3.)

Romans 8.5–8   The Great Antithesis

There are two kinds of life, the life which ends in death, introverted, self-centred, seeking all its satisfaction in the pursuit and fulfilment of the passing and ephemeral desires of the body. Opposed to it, and as different as life is from death (Eph. 2.1–6), is the 'eternal life' of which John, writing thirty to forty years later, speaks, the life which seeks God's will, outward-going, free, conscious of God's presence, help, upholding, the life available to all who will lay hold of it in faith.

The Lord told the story of a fool (Luke 12.15–23). The man was a farmer, no monster of wickedness. In a difficult land, he had made farming pay. There is no suggestion that he had won wealth by any means other than hard work. But he mistook his body for his soul. He thought life needed only a heap of wheat and farm produce. He

45

thought he could control the future. He illustrates v. 6. He was typical of those who live according to the flesh. Such a life is, as Shakespeare made Macbeth describe it, 'a brief candle'—

> *'Life's but a walking shadow, a poor player,*
> *That struts and frets his hour upon the stage*
> *And then is heard no more; it is a tale*
> *Told by an idiot, full of sound and fury.*
> *Signifying nothing . . .'*

Such is not the life 'in Christ'. Paul exhausts metaphor in his attempt to make clear and challenging the difference. We have quoted Eph. **2**. Look at the first four verses of Col. **3** with its climax in vs. 3 f.: 'You have died, and your life is hidden with Christ in God, and when Christ, who has become our very being, shall appear, then you shall share His glory.' Or as Phillips renders: '. . . Christ, the secret centre of our lives . . .'

Look, too, at Phil. **3**.12–16 where Paul makes it quite clear that the life 'in Christ', the life 'according to the Spirit', is no effortless or sudden transformation. It is attained by growing and continually exercised faith, by 'abiding'. 'He must go on increasing, and I must go on decreasing', said John the Baptist, if his words may be translated with due stress on the present infinitives in the text. They express continuity, a process, and contain a deep Christian truth (John 3.30). Our 'brief candle' merges its flicker with the unquenchable 'Light of the World'.

Romans 8.9–11 Risen with Christ

Observe how vital in Paul's teaching is the truth of the resurrection. To believe in the historic fact of the resurrection is essential for a Christian faith. The name Christian cannot properly be given to anyone denying the deep truth of that event. To be sure it is, as these verses show, a mystical experience, part of living 'in Christ'. But that experience loses all meaning if Christ be not truly risen. It is the apprehension of the fact, the realization that He did indeed conquer death, which makes possible the basic affirmation: 'My Lord and my God!'.

Thomas was the last of the apostles' band to see the risen Christ, and he was no man to hazard life on a false report, mistake, hallucination or fabrication. Remembering the census documents of the eastern provinces, where identification is often made by reference to permanent scars, he said: 'Unless I put my finger into the print of the nails, and my hand into the spear wound in His side, I will not believe.' Such were Christ's identifying scars, and such demonstration Christ offered the doubter. 'My Lord,' cried the broken man, 'and my God!' Catch what J. B. Phillips in his well-known little book called the 'ring of truth' in the breathless simplicity of that affirmation. 'Blessed,' said Christ, 'are those who have not seen and yet believe.'

'Hath He marks to lead me to Him?' asks Stephen of Saba in the hymn which he built round Thomas' experience. He has, indeed, His marks, marks on all history, marks on countless transformed lives, and He still calls for Thomas' affirmation. No despite is done to reason in making it. Once it is made, life can never be the same again. Such committal involves all life, penetrates the whole person. . . . In Greece, at Easter, the cry goes up: 'Christ is risen', and for forty days no other greeting of welcome or farewell is used, only the one triumphant proclamation. Thus the Greek Christian signifies that no activity of life, no movement of the mind, no plan of work, no project of pleasure, indeed, no pain, no joy, no sorrow, no speech, no thought, lies outside the scope of an embracing faith. And unless Christ be risen there is no Christianity, all hope is cut at the root, the foundation of all goodness sapped . . . More. The indwelling Spirit is that of Him who raised Jesus from the dead (11), and therefore immortality is also assured.

Romans 8.12–17   The Indwelling Presence

The theme continually returns to the Christian's intimations of immortality. It is because the eternal Spirit of God indwells the Christian that his survival is assured. It is because he is one with the Risen Lord that he will share in that resurrection.

Other implications follow. If God's Spirit lives in the Christian, the mind of God should be discerned by the Christian, and God's guidance should be his common experience. This guidance, be it understood, does not suspend or override his judgement and reason but informs both, leading to sanctified discernment between right and wrong. Guidance, in a thousand situations, needs no more than that clear knowledge. At that point God's way becomes obvious.

We thus return to the thought that has been implicit in much of what Paul has already written—that life for the Christian is a process of renewal, a moving towards reality. First comes by faith the knowledge that God Himself has penetrated the very person, the 'heart' of the Biblical imagery. Then comes realization of that continuing fact, deeper daily committal to all that it implies of present wisdom, enveloping love, and increasing power—until at last we become like Him, lost in Him, and yet, paradoxically, more ourselves, our true selves, more alive than ever we could have been lost in death. Such is the redemption of the personality.

Inevitably the body dies, but the body is not all. It is the end which counts in all that has to do with man, whom God made 'in His image'. Reviewing twenty years ago Professor Butterfield's *Christianity and History*, McEwan Lawson wrote: 'There is a habit in this machine age of thinking we have explained everything when we have stated its origin . . . Long ago Aristotle pointed out that for the full explanation of anything you have to look not only at its origin but at its goal. An oak springs from an acorn, but it springs from an acorn so that it may reach air and sun . . . A man may begin humbly enough, but his explanation is only complete when you can see that the goal of his journey is festooned by stars.' Such is 'the blessed hope',

> *'with this elate*
> *Let not our souls be desolate . . .*
> *But strong in faith in patience wait*
> *Until He come.'*

Meditation: 2 Cor. **4**.16.

Notes: V. 15: 'spirit of sonship' should probably read 'Spirit . . .' as in the AV(KJV), NEB. The Spirit of the Son is given to the Christians (Gal. **4**.6). V. 17: Note the Christian's identification with Christ as heirs of God (cf. Matt. **21**.38; **25**.34) and as those who suffer (cf. 2 Tim. **2**.11 f.; 2 Cor. **1**.5; **4**.10; Phil. **3**.10 f.).

Romans 8.18–21 Ravaged World

In yesterday's note the figure of adoption was not stressed because it means less in the modern social context than it did in the ancient world. F. H. Palmer's article in the *New Bible Dictionary* provides material for those interested in the metaphor.

But we must pause here to mark the triumphant point Paul has reached in his developing argument. By adoption the child of God is made absolutely and completely a member of God's family. The sharer of its privileges, the partaker in its life.

Then abruptly he brings the subject back to earth, for man, after all, sure though his heritage may be, is here on earth, this dying planet, this polluted world. The adopted child of God must endure, in a spoiled and alien environment, all manner of testing until God claims His own.

The argument then begins to tangle with a piece of extraordinary insight. That the very planet suffered in man is implicit in the O.T.

(Gen. **3**.17; Isa. **11**.9). Paul pictures the ravaged globe, and the suffering of its humbler creatures finding pause and healing in God's consummation of His creative and redeeming project.

'We must make peace with nature,' said President Nixon in his 'state of the union' address in January 1970, but no peace can be made with nature, save by those who make their peace with God. How menacingly demonstrable is the truth that man involved the planet in his fall and ruin. Man's mastery of nature shares the bend and twist which sin has given to all man's other God-given qualities. In the hands of a rebellious creature it has become a force of destruction. C. S. Lewis pictured the Un-man in *Perelandra* walking through the newly-created Paradise, and tearing open the coloured frogs, ripping leaf and flower from the trees, destroying, sadistically, instinctively. In exact proportion to his 'progress', 'culture', 'civilization', man has become a devouring force before whose onslaught nature has wilted. During three to ten centuries nature can build an inch of fertile topsoil. During one reckless century man has used up, over vital areas of the world's surface, all nature's stored resources. Greedy farming and selfish exploitation have taken no thought for the morrow. Hence bared hills, choked streams, dust-bowls, famine, disaster, polluted air, fouled rivers and dead lakes, as nature answers back. 'The whole creation has been groaning in travail' because of man. Why, when all else forms a scheme harmonious, does man give the impression of disharmony? Why does he act like a brutal nomad in occupation of lands not his own? Why seek further than the penetrating explanation behind the Genesis story? Man fell, and from his fall came his pain, his toil, his exile.

Romans 8.22–25 Hope

Yesterday's note overflowed into v. 22. In Christ lies the hope for all creation. Verses 19–22 speak of the sighing of the world under the feet of its rebel occupants. In vs. 23–25 is the yearning hope of the Christians themselves. A third section follows which will form the next note, vs. 26 f., which tell the rich truth of the Spirit's intercession.

The 'first fruits of the Spirit', that earnest of God's presence, only sharpens the hope of full emancipation, makes the Christian at times feel an alien in a strange land, a citizen of heaven exiled on earth. (See 1 Cor. **15**.53–58; 2 Cor. **5**.2; Phil. **3**.21 for the line of thought, and, for the same teaching about the Spirit under a different figure of speech, 2 Cor. **1**.22; **5**.5; Eph. **1**.14.)

The theme of hope then takes over. Hope is inherent in our

salvation. At times, in the stress of circumstance, hope is all we have. Faith engenders it. The alternative is despair, and despair is rampant around us. Without Christ what hope is there for man? Without a return to Christ what solution is there for the mounting problems of society? H. G. Wells, who began life as an optimist, ended with the abandonment of his conception of a society evolving by technology and science into the glory of a millennial peace and plenty. He ended with 'Man at the End of His Tether' dying 'in the disease-soaked ruins of a slum'.

Where there is no hope there can be no endeavour, and denied hope, as some would deny men hope, the vital energies of civilization will decay. Whatever enlarges hope exalts courage and endurance (25), and nerves men to face difficulty and testing. Undermine hope by undermining faith, and the spirit of man will wither. Faith and hope infuse love (1 Cor. 13.13). Let both decay, and love dies, and if love dies the world dies, submerged in selfishness and hate. And what hope can there be if death is finally supreme—death for man, and the 'vast death of the solar system', of the late Bertrand Russell's despairing phrase?

> Meditation: 'Whether we be young or old,
>   Our destiny, our being's heart and home,
>   Is with infinitude, and only there;
>   With hope it is, hope that can never die,
>   Effort and expectation and desire,
>   And something evermore about to be'
>
>   (Wordsworth, The Prelude 6.603 ff.).

Questions for further study and discussion on Romans chs. 7.21—8.25

1. What principles of Christian preaching derive from Paul's evident personal involvement in his theme?
2. Did Nicodemus understand, from his great knowledge of the O.T., what the Lord said about rebirth?
3. What is life to you?
4. What is involved in immortality, and why does the Christian believe in it?
5. Why are faith, hope and love linked? (1 Thess, 1.3; 5.8; Gal. 5.5 f.; 1 Cor. 13.13; Heb. 6.10–12; 1 Pet. 1.21 f.).
6. What is the significance of 4.18 and 5.5 in the light of Paul's teaching on hope?

The third testimony forms one of the gems of Scripture. Prayer is the life-blood of faith. The Lord prayed, sometimes the night through in times of spiritual crisis, and no one can be truly Christian who does not, by the instinctive uplifting of the heart, seek God's aid in times of menace, stress, difficulty and temptation.

But, in the light of these verses, let two deep truths be realized. First, as Archbishop Trench said: 'Prayer is not overcoming God's reluctance, it is laying hold of God's willingness.' If the Spirit indwells the Christian, and that has been the chapter's insistent theme, then God's mind mingles with ours in our prayers. R. W. Dale has a striking comment on the passage before us which under-lines this thought. It illustrates, he wrote, 'in a startling manner the truth and reality of the coming of the Holy Spirit—the extent to which, if I may venture to say it, He has separated Himself—as Christ did at His incarnation—from His eternal glory and blessed-ness, and entered into the life of man. His intercession for us—so intimately does He share all the evils of our condition—is a kind of *agony*'.

Secondly, note that, clear and coherent, and indeed, specific, as we should be in the framing of our prayers, we cannot, being ignorant of the future, know precisely that for which we should properly pray. God answers prayer, and that is the experience of all Christ-ians, not always in accordance with the garbled specifications of the petitioner, but in ways infinitely more subtle, more rewarding and wise. Sometimes, in times of stress, failure and strife, there is nothing else to do but bow in surrender, commit whatever it is, or whatever has happened, to the eternal wisdom and love, and to leave God Himself to phrase petitions that we could only phrase if we knew all, and could foresee all. C. H. Dodd puts it thus: 'Prayer is the Divine in us appealing to the Divine above us', but it is more than that. It is a surge of faith born of His Presence in the heart, and confident of an answer because the uplift of the needy heart cannot be other than the prompting of God. It is such a resource and refuge, in a God whom He called Father, that Christ gave to men in the Lord's Prayer.

Meditation: 'I have been driven many times to my knees by the overwhelming conviction that I had nowhere else to go. My own wisdom, and that of all about me, seemed insufficient for the day' (Abraham Lincoln).

Two themes are here apparent: (*i*) *God's Plan*. It is logical to believe that, if our lives are committed to the guidance and government of Perfect Love, then Love, which is God (1 John 4.8), will desire our ultimate and perfect happiness. And if our lives are controlled by Perfect Wisdom, then God, who is omniscient and makes no mistakes, can plan and perfect our happiness. The only limiting factor is our will. How completely can we or do we commit our lives to the Power who, in perfect love and perfect wisdom, can secure our ultimate felicity, usefulness and content? It also follows that any experience committed to God, whether it be pain or pleasure, good or evil, can be woven into the pattern for good. Phillips' rendering: 'everything that happens fits into a pattern for good', brings out the point that nothing, even failure and sin, is exempt from God's transforming beneficence if it is, in complete faith, surrendered to His creative hands.

(*ii*) *Predestination.* Let it be realized that this solemn subject eludes our comprehension. Theologians, from Augustine to Calvin and today, have sought to reduce to logical synthesis the facts of God's foreknowledge and human freedom. It cannot be done without leaving natural questionings about ultimate love and justice which cannot be shrugged off. It is useless to say that 'in the course of justice none of us would see salvation', that 'because grace is grace none of us is entitled to it', that 'no one can demand that God should give an account of the principles on which He bestows His grace' . . . All these statements are quite true but will not satisfy those who see what Barclay calls 'a strange and terrible selectiveness' in it all. Barclay, in fact, cuts through much dangerous and baffling speculation when he refuses to take this passage as either a considered statement of theology or a piece of Christian philosophy, but rather the lyrical expression of a mature facet of Christian experience. When a Christian looks back over the course of his life, conscious though he is that he has decided of his own free will again and again at vital moments of crisis or encounter, there is all along the solemn conviction that God was at work. How the blend of human and divine is effected no one knows or will know this side of heaven, but to look at the passage as lyric testimony leaves the mind at peace and praising, not crushed and daunted by sombre thoughts of God.

The lyric mood continues as Paul rides his wave of exultation. With a clear reference to the story of Abraham's ultimate demonstration of faithfulness (32; Gen. **22.**16), Paul speaks of God's tremendous exhibition of His care for man. At the cross of Christ God finally revealed His nature. He was 'in Christ reconciling the world to Himself'. If He could suffer thus to convince and save, how true must be the opening words of the chapter! There can be 'no condemnation' in time or eternity, if God has gone to this length to redeem.

Who alone could condemn? Only Christ, who lived as man to qualify beyond all human disputation for the role of judge, and through whom in consequence, God will indeed judge 'the quick and the dead at His appearing'. But see, for those who trust Him, Christ sits not as judge but as intercessor. Phillips renders this triumphant passage well: 'Who would dare to accuse us, whom God has chosen? The judge Himself has declared us free from sin. Who is in a position to condemn? Only Christ, and Christ died for us, Christ rose for us, Christ reigns in power for us, Christ prays for us' (Acts **17.**31; Heb. **9.**27).

It is interesting to see Paul's mind; in the fervour of this grand passage, working within the context of Scripture and the oral tradition of the yet unwritten words of Christ. We have already pointed out the reference to Gen. **22.** Observe also Matt. **6.**33; Isa. **50.**8 f.; **52.**13–**53.**12; Psa. **110.**1. A mind soaked in the O.T. Scriptures finds mode and framework for thought and its expression in remembered text and situation, allusion and echo.

Here then is Christian security, the last ground of assurance, that essential to peace and poise. It is Jesus Christ, 'at God's right hand', with the atoning death a fact of history, and pleading His people's cause. The imagery is, of course, that of a royal court, but the word-picture is vivid and complete—'bold we approach the eternal throne . . .' See also Heb. **7.**25; **9.**24; 1 John **2.**1 f.

And it is all of faith, for Paul's major theme is still implicit.

Meditation: 'Faith is the root of all blessings. Believe, and you shall be saved; believe, and you must needs be satisfied; believe and you cannot but be comforted and happy' (Jeremy Taylor).

Romans 8.35–39   Triumphant Ending

The somewhat over-conservative rendering of the RSV does not do justice to the power and poetry of Paul's conclusion. Both Phillips and the NEB catch its spirit well. We shall look at each verse in turn:

Verse 35. The physical trials listed are those of Paul's own experience. Look at other autobiographical passages—2 Cor. 6.4–10; 11.24–27; 12.10.

Verse 36. The mention of the 'sword' suggests to Paul, steeped as he is in the O.T., the words of Psa. 44.22, which is quoted exactly as it stands in the Greek Bible, the Septuagint. But note the transformation. The psalmist, in bleak despair, expostulates with God. He could understand how men could suffer for sin, or for abandonment of God, but not 'for God's sake', for fidelity and truth. Paul understood. To suffer for Christ's sake was to enter into the fellowship of His sufferings, and to be honoured by the blessed partnership (5.2; 2 Cor. 1.5; Col. 1.24).

Verse 37. The word so happily rendered 'more than conquerors' was perhaps a poetic coinage of Paul's. The RSV was wise to retain it from the AV(KJV). The Christian is pictured as no battered and exhausted victor, but as a confident, triumphant conqueror.

Verse 38. The opening verb is that of 2 Tim. 1.12: 'I . . . am persuaded . . .' (AV[KJV]). Then come the powerful alternatives. Life is often more difficult to face than death. Christ conquered death. He also conquered life, and our life is hidden with Him (John 8.51; 10.28; 11.25; 2 Cor. 4.16—5.5; Heb. 2.14 f.). 'Angels . . . principalities . . . powers' are probably the spiritual forces against which the Christian wars (Eph. 6.12). These hostile powers which lie behind the material universe have already been defeated by Christ (Col. 2.15; 1 Pet. 3.22). Phillips' rendering 'neither messenger of heaven nor monarch of earth' may be correct. The remaining alternatives, 'things present . . . things to come', are understandable in the experience of everyone.

Verse 39. Summing up, Paul repeats v. 35. He has spoken of the dimensions of time (38). Rhetorically he adds the dimensions of space, and then grasps the very universe. Nothing, no, nothing, can divide the child of God from his Father.

    Meditation: '*Thou wilt keep him in peace, PEACE . . .*' (Isa.
                  26.3—literally).
                '*. . . the future all unknown—Jesus we know, and*
                He is on the throne.'

Romans 9.1–5   The Jews

A positive exposition of the gospel has occupied the first eight chapters of the letter, and concluded on a high note of faith. This chapter introduces a new theme. It has been reasonably suggested that chs. 9 —11 form a distinct and coherent unit because they are, in fact, an address which Paul habitually gave to synagogue congregations wholly composed of Jews. Yet there is a connection with what goes before. Paul finds it necessary to answer a question which would puzzle many of his readers. How was this new message of righteousness and salvation apart from the Law consistent with the privileged position of the Jewish nation? Had God rejected them? Was He inconsistent?

Thus this section is intimately woven into the structure of the epistle. Paul had himself passed through an agonizing reappraisal of all that Judaism meant to him, and all Christians of Jewish birth and upbringing had similarly to reassess a lifetime of belief and thinking. They had to realize that their cherished heritage was not an end in itself but a means to an end, not final and complete, but a preparation destined to find consummation, completion and submersion in a fuller revelation.

The bulk of Jewry found the adjustment impossible. Hence a grim dilemma of daunting magnitude for all who treasured Judaism. Hence the passionate attempts to absorb Christianity and make it a reforming sect of Judaism. The Messiah, as was expected, came from the Jews, but, if Paul preached Christ's message aright, the Messiah brought condemnation, not redemption, to the mass of the 'chosen people'. In short, the Jew protested, if the Christian Church represented the consummation of God's plan for the world, then God appeared to deny all that He had owned and to have broken the ancient covenant with Israel.

This, to any devout Jew, would have seemed impossible. It followed that the preaching of Paul must be rejected as mistaken or perverse. Paul had passed through the stress of this dilemma. He had seen with God's own clarity that there was no contradiction. Since his first audience everywhere was Jewish, it was essential for him to speak convincingly of this difficult theme. The next three chapters are his argument.

The first five verses show how he loved his blinded compatriots. Then, from 9.6–29 Paul asserts the sovereignty of God. The Jew had no special claim on God. Next, from **9.30—10.**21 Paul boldly avers that the Jews' rejection by God is the result of their own wilful stubbornness. In ch. **11** he shows how the ingathering of the Gentiles made the ancient promise real.

Romans 9.6–9   True Israel

Is then God's plan defeated, if those who, as a people, gave Christ to the world, have rejected Him? Not at all. Paul appeals to all the range of history. Embedded in the events of the earliest covenant is a principle of choice. 'Abraham's children', the race of the promise, were those of one line, that of Isaac. Ishmael was equally a son of Abraham, but had no part in the lineage of the covenant (Gen. **21.**12). The real descent was not as man, but as God, ordained it (Gen. **18.**10–14), with the accompaniment of special overruling, and in a context of miracle.

It was therefore established, even in the time of the patriarch, that a selected line was that which should carry Abraham's name. It was not merely physical descent that should be the determining factor. The word (6) in virtue of which Isaac was born was a word of 'promise' (8 f.). He was 'born from above', and there is no other way of becoming 'a child of God' (8) save by such a process. Gal. **4.**28 calls Christians 'children of promise', like Isaac. It therefore follows that the privilege of such sonship is open to Gentiles as well as to Jews. Observe the bold reasoning by which Paul attaches the right of the Gentile to salvation to the most ancient covenant of the Jew. If we are Christ's, we are also Abraham's descendants.

It had, in fact, been implicit in the whole situation. Abraham, on the great historic occasion, had been bidden to observe the sands of the surrounding desert as a picture of his posterity. He had been told to regard the stars of heaven, although it is only in the present century that man has known that their multitude is comparable with the desert's sand. Here, in poetic imagery, is the suggestion of a twin posterity—earthly and heavenly.

The climate of thought has changed. We see no difficulty in the theme of Abraham's posterity. A 'chosen people', in the narrow Jewish sense, would be *our* stumbling block. Paul's careful argument demonstrates the different historical situation in which his evangelism was cast. Those scholars who maintain that the Roman church to which Paul wrote was synagogue-based, and partially Jewish, are probably correct. Paul's argument would seem logical to them. At least it fell within the pattern of their common dialectic.

And from that thought emerges another. God is ready to meet us on the level of our preoccupations, to move within the framework of our thoughts. And that should be the endeavour of our own evangelism—to meet men and women where they think or understand, however perverse sometimes such habits of thinking may appear to us.

Questions for further study and discussion on Romans chs. 8.26—9.9

1. How does faith enter into prayer?
2. How does the great hymn: 'O Love, that wilt not let me go', illustrate the synthesis of God's action in a human life and man's freedom of will?

3. 'The pattern of fear changes from century to century, but not fear's remedy.' Discuss this.
4. Why were the Jews 'chosen'?
5. What were 'the covenants'? How did the Jews misconstrue them?
6. Can you discern reasons for God's choice of Isaac and Jacob?

Romans 9.10–13 Further Illustration

In a further movement of argument which would appear relevant to the Jews whom he addressed, Paul moves forward one generation in the story of the patriarchs. Paul pictures his Jewish opponent observing that Ishmael was discarded because it was in observance of a pagan custom that Abraham took Hagar, and that Hagar was a slave and an alien. He was therefore illegitimate, and could not rank in privilege with Sarah's son. But 'we are Abraham's seed and were never in bondage to any man' (John **8**.33–39).

In answer Paul points to Isaac's children, where no distinction of paternal fault or conduct, no difference of racial background, could be alleged. The two children, Esau and Jacob, were twins. Before there could be any visible grounds of choice between them on the basis of conduct, it was pronounced that the elder, by a few minutes, should serve the younger. God, in His sovereign will, rejected Esau. (Paul has in mind the opening verses of Malachi.)

Note very carefully that God is speaking of Esau and Jacob in relation to the heritage, the carrying on of the covenanted line of God's people. He is not discussing the eternal salvation or perdition of individual men and women in accordance with an absolute and pre-natal decree of God exercised without relation to their will or works, and resting solely upon an inscrutable and incomprehensible will. His object is to preclude the idea that man has claims against God, and, after his own characteristically intense fashion of argument, he pursues it singlemindedly.

He is urgent to establish the fact that the visible exclusion of a great mass of contemporary Jewry from the kingdom of their own Messiah was no breach of faith on the part of the Almighty towards the posterity of Abraham. Always, His purpose has run through an inner group—the Remnant. Paul pauses before the opaque veil of God's will. But, in Moule's phrase, 'he knows that only righteousness and love are behind it; but he knows that it *is* a veil, and that in front of it man's thought must cease and be silent'.

Note: Malachi's theme (**1**.2 f.) is the *nations* of Israel and Edom, not the individual ancestors of those nations, Jacob and Esau.

Israel was the elect nation, who suffered inhumanity from the hands of its 'brother' Edom. 'Hated' is a Hebraism. Edom certainly fell under judgement (Psa. **137**.7; Isa. **34**.5 ff.; Jer. **49**.7 ff.).

Romans 9.14–16

We have pointed out that it was a habit of Paul in argument to pursue one end with ruthless logic. Consequently, to take a verse or a section of an argument out of its context may be to distort truth. Scripture must be taken as a whole, and statement balanced and conditioned by statement.

Now, if Paul's words are considered without these precautions, he would appear to be saying that God can do exactly what He wishes, and no man can question His justice, and secondly, that men can desire salvation with the passion and purpose of one who runs to win a race, and yet be denied it, because, without shred of explanation, God has decreed otherwise.

This cannot be true. First, although God is omnipotent, He cannot act in any way contrary to His nature. He is perfect love, and He cannot act otherwise than in love. He is ultimate justice, and cannot do other than justly. 'Shall not the Judge of all the earth do right?' said Abraham in a phrase of immortal insight. He is perfect wisdom, and cannot do other than wisely.

Secondly, consider the breadth and balance of our Lord's statements. Recognizing the work of His Father, He states a complementary truth '. . . him who comes to Me I will not (under any circumstances) reject' (John **6**.37). (The parenthesis attempts to do justice to the emphatic Greek negatives.) His invitation goes to all who will respond: 'Come to Me, all who labour . . .' (Matt. **11**.28).

Thirdly, consider F. F. Bruce's wise remarks (*Tyndale N.T. Commentary on Romans*, pp. 190, 191): 'It is a pity that in some schools of theological thought the doctrine of election has been formulated to an excessive degree on the basis of this preliminary stage in Paul's present argument, without adequate account being taken of his further exposition of God's purpose in election at the close of the argument (**11**.25–32) . . . In point of fact, as appears with blessed clarity later in the present argument, God's grace is far wider than anyone could have dared to hope . . . For centuries the Gentiles had been looked upon by the chosen people, with but a few exceptions, as "vessels of wrath fitted for destruction", and certainly God had "endured" them "with much longsuffering"; but now the purpose of His patience was made plain; what He desired was not their doom but their salvation.'

58

Meditation: 'See in thy choice of Him His mercy on thee. And now fall at His feet and bless Him, serve Him and trust Him. Think ill of thyself and reverently of others. And remember He "willeth not the death of a sinner", He loved the world, He bids thee tell it that He loved it, to tell it that He is Love' (Handley Moule).

Romans 9.17–20   The Case of Pharaoh

The relevant chapters of the Exodus story should be read again. Seen as human history, it was apparent that the ruler of Egypt was a tyrant, who repeatedly and capriciously changed his policy, and fought with dogged and arrogant persistence against justice and human rights, and also against fearsome natural phenomena, which he was assured demonstrated the power and urgency of God pressing upon him. He was clearly a self-willed, evil and obstinate man determined to deny justice to a race of trampled slaves.

When the Bible says that God 'hardened Pharaoh's heart', it does not mean that here was a human being who might have surrendered and done righteously, had not God deliberately frustrated his desire for good, and headed His unfortunate victim in the direction of evil. It would violate the very nature of God, and make Him like sinful man if God could be imagined forcing a human soul to do evil, or in any way blocking a desire to do good.

Pharaoh willed it all. What then does the strange phrase mean? It means that God initiated and set in motion those moral and psychological laws which Pharaoh refused to recognize. One of those laws is that, when a mind sets itself with determination to do evil, the very choice makes it more easy to do evil. When, in rebellious self-will, a man places himself in opposition to God, each moment's persistence promotes the death of conscience, and makes the road to retreat and to penitence longer and more difficult. Hebrew thought does not distinguish the intermediate steps. God created the laws of the mind. Therefore, said the Jew, God 'hardened Pharaoh's heart'.

God permitted Pharaoh, a prominent and historic example of defiant sin, to pursue his disastrous course, in order to demonstrate to Egyptian and Jew alike that God cannot be defied with impunity. Pharaoh willed it thus. God sentenced him to go on his chosen course of wickedness, and used him as a warning beacon at its ending. Grim is the fate of the man to whom God says: 'Thy will be done.'

'Pharaoh's case,' says Bishop Moule, 'was a case of concurrent phenomena. *A man* there was on the one hand, willingly, deliberately, and most guiltily battling with right, and rightly bringing ruin on his own head, wholly of himself. *God* there was on the other hand, making that man a monument, not of grace but of judgement. And that side, that line, is isolated here, and treated as if it were all.'

It is a further example of the single-mindedness of Paul's style of argument.

Romans 9.21–24   'Vessels of Wrath'

Paul took his imagery of the pot from Jer. **18.**1–6. It is another example of his habit of driving the argument along one line to one specific conclusion, without care for derivative notions. He is asserting with vigour that the gulf between the intelligence of God and that of man is so vast that it is absurd to argue with Him. It is the thought of Psa. **2.**2–4.

On the other hand a human being is not an insentient pot, and Paul would have been the first to stress the fact that one for whom Christ died was not dead clay. Man is born to question and to seek, and God is ready in the course of time to supply the answer. Pots are not made in their Creator's image, and it is precisely because man bears the lineaments of the divine that he does, and may, answer God. Job and Jeremiah call aloud for the justification of God's ways to man. Read the psalms, and the psalm Christ quoted (**22.**1).

The passage cannot mean that God creates human beings capable of suffering in order to make them suffer, and to punish them for that which eludes their control. Such a God is not the God of either O.T. or N.T. On the other hand God can reject or choose man or nation for this or that piece of work in the ordered scheme of history, and this is the thought uppermost in Paul's mind as he wrestles with the problem of Israel's rejection, and their strange hostility to their Messiah.

There is also, as F. F. Bruce points out, the defiant answering back of rebellion and disobedience, and distinct from the questioning of faithful bewilderment. Nor does this conclude the argument. In the third section of the theme Paul exhibits the will of God as exercised in such a manner that no reproach, however presumptuous, can be urged against it. Moreover, is not the fact that God withholds adverse action, asserted in vs. 22 f., sufficient indication that, even in this context of argument, Paul looks upon 'the vessels of wrath' as responsible beings who need time to repent, and that, in turn, implies the capability of repentance? 'The "wrath" of the Holy

One,' says Handley Moule, 'can fall only upon demerit, so these "vessels" have merited His displeasure of themselves . . . sin is altogether "of" the creature.'

Romans 9.25–29   The Remnant

The continuation in these verses of the austere and difficult passage which formed yesterday's study shows how completely the theme of Israel's rejection, and Israel's disobedience, dominated Paul's mind. And interwoven with that appears the thought that it was the wideness, not the narrowness of God's mercy which was prominent in his mind, for was not the fulfilment of two prophecies of Hosea visible before their eyes? The despised, and too often hated, Gentiles were the recipients of God's favour (Hos. 2.23; 1.10; 1 Pet. 2.10).

He pursues the same line of thought into the prophecy of Isaiah. The prophet foresaw dire days of tribulation falling upon his land, and such decimation of his people that 'a remnant' only would survive to carry on the national task and the divine tradition. He touched in this statement a principle of divine action, which we have already noticed, almost a principle of history—that it is 'the Few' who bring salvation (Isa. 7,8; 10.21 f.).

Historically that catastrophe, and its associated triumph, came to pass. Israel *was* ravaged. A remnant only were able to rebuild the land and rescue and preserve the national heritage. And so, Paul saw, it was happening again. A remnant only had open eyes. A few, a blessed few, recognized God's visitation in Christ. Observe the subtlety of Paul's argument, and compare it with the controversial tactics of Christ Himself in His confrontation with scribes and Pharisees. Such was the reverence paid to the text of Scripture that an oracle quoted from a prophetic authority was considered sufficient answer. Compare the form of argument in the Epistle to the Hebrews.

In neither the Lord's case, nor Paul's, of course, was this form of refutation without relevance. In the prophets, notably in Isaiah, the global nature of the Messiah's role, and the Gentile part in a world theocracy, were clearly foreseen. We have already noted the hint of a spiritual posterity for Abraham in the imagery of the stars. Note, too, the role of the N.T. in enlarging the earlier application of an O.T. passage. In both the Hosea quotations the immediate application of the words is to the restoration of the Ten Tribes to their covenanted blessing. Paul sees, and extracts, a wider significance of the principle involved, the inclusion of all the rebels of mankind in the same circle of beneficence. The Word is living, and in its interpretation (from an understanding of the Apocalypse to the use of the Bible in personal devotion) meaning is not confined to one significance, one area of truth and challenge.

Romans 9.30–33   The Stumbling-Stone

How strange the paradox! The prepared, the endowed, the children of promise and covenant, fail to grasp the consummation of all their history, the final significance of all their God had done for them, while those remote from the plan which outworked through Israel's history see, in a burst of sudden glory, the meaning of Christ, and enter into His salvation. It left Paul shocked and crushed but thrilled. But the explanation lay close to hand. Israel lacked faith. The Gentiles who accepted Christ had faith. It was as simple as that.

So this closely-woven chapter concludes. It is the attempt of a 'Hebrew of the Hebrews' to explain that which was a fearful problem for those of his race who were attracted to Christ, but who felt that the by-passing of Israel was tantamount to a break of ancient and sacred covenants. We have seen the main points now of Paul's solution: (i) The Jew thought that absolute obedience to the Law set him right with God; (ii) Paul, in his own living experience, had found the Law impossible to keep; (iii) the Law, therefore, being undoubtedly of God, had another function. It was incomplete, a preparation for Christ; (iv) Christ saved by faith, a gift of grace which the Law could not bestow; (v) and if Christ thus forgave, it followed that the Gentile who received Him, though he had lacked the preparation and advantage of the Jew, was received in Christ; (vi) it also followed that the Jew who rejected Christ was lost, and had no claim on God whatever. Hence the terrible dilemma.

So Christ became a stumbling-block for the Jews. He was the foundation stone of God's new structure (Matt. **21**.42; Psa. **118**.22; Isa. **8**.14; **28**.16; Acts **4**.11; Eph. **2**.20; 1 Pet. **2**.4–8). The N.T. was fond of elaborating the image. That which was intended to be the very basis and understanding of salvation became a barrier in the path, a 'rock of offence' (33, AV[KJV]) to those who refused to place it in the proper position.

The closing words are a precious promise. Those who stand firm upon the foundation 'other than which no man can lay' will not find their confidence ill-founded. The raging flood of the Isaian passage will pass by, turbid with the world's chaos, but he will stand, and 'having done all still stand'.

Here begins the second section of Paul's 'Synagogue Sermon'. He has demonstrated that Israel has no claim, and right, to special treatment. Their whole history, rightly conceived, showed God acting towards man on principles quite alien from those to which they clung with such fervour. He is now about to show that this grave and fundamental error was made in self-will, but before launching this indictment he feels compelled, in anguish of heart, to cry aloud his concern and love for his people. (Read again 9.30–33, which are continued here, and might logically have been included in this chapter.)

Observe that he speaks of the Jews in the third person, an indication that he regards the Roman Christian community ('brethren') as a people apart, and not entirely Jewish in their ethnic content. The nature of his argument, so preoccupied with the imagined righteousness of the Law, and the assumption of a full and detailed knowledge of the covenants, is surely proof that the Church in Rome was not, as some contend, on the strength of this third person pronoun, completely Gentile.

But the deepest interest of these verses is their biographical content. They reveal the Christlikeness of Paul. Like his Master, he 'weeps over Jerusalem'. He has said stern things about the Jews. He is about to say more, and to press home with insistence the charge of wilful rebellion. But he does it with yearning, not anger. He pleads; he does not denounce. Read Ezek. 3.14–21. Commissioned to speak grim words to the exiles of Israel, the prophet went 'in bitterness in the heat of his spirit' to the labour camp on the great Chebar irrigation canal. And 'the hand of the Lord' fell upon him, and he 'sat where they sat' (AV[KJV]) seven days. Having shared the misery of those to whom he was to minister, he was at last allowed to speak, and did so, with no less regard for truth, but deeper understanding. Paul had already 'sat where they sat' (Phil. 3.4–6), and it is out of that fellowship of blindness, in the sharp memory of his Pharisaic sin, that he speaks the words of this epistle. It is a model for preachers. Let there be none of the denunciation which hardens and speaks of self-righteousness, no hard castigating of sinners, but rather the indictment of sin, and in all, and through all, the love of Christ constraining.

Romans 10.5–8   Righteousness not to be Achieved

Paul's argument now resorts to the quotation of authoritative texts of Scripture, such as we have seen him do before, and which is surely evidence that he was addressing a congregation familiar both with this use of Scripture and the O.T. Furthermore, the clause by clause exposition of the second passage, which Paul quotes, is in the style of some of the commentaries in the Dead Sea Scrolls.

To our mind neither quotation seems, on the surface of the words, to support Paul's argument. It seems therefore to follow that the Christian Church was already familiar with the new interpretation of the verses concerned. This appears to be especially the case with the second passage, which, on the face of it, seems to bear something of the same meaning as the first. Paul turns it into an allegory of Christ, so briefly as to leave the impression that his hearers must have heard the interpretation before.

Consider the two passages: (*i*) Lev. **18.**5. Moses was the author of the Law. He states that the man who performs its statutes shall live thereby. That is precisely what the bewildered Jew said he was doing. But Paul has been to tremendous pains to prove that such self-confidence was based on a defective view of performance, and a lamentably faulty view of sin. To keep the Law, and to 'live' by doing so, was the aim of every 'Israelite indeed'. But even before Christ came, it must have been an endeavour conscious of its inadequacy, with calling on God to aid, lift and forgive. Paul is aiming his words rather at the Pharisee and legalist, who claimed perfection, and full achievement. 'Keep the Law and live.' 'But the Law cannot be kept' (Gal. **3.**10–12).

(*ii*) Deut. **30.**11–14. Paul is not so much quoting this eloquent passage as basing upon its words a free interpretation which makes them a prophecy of Christ. The passage, in fact, meant that the Law was near and practicable, but always assuming a context of repentance and awareness of sin, and indeed, in the remote ancient setting, a remedy of ritual and sacrifice. Paul sets the passage in the context of his own argument, and his wider conviction that the Law only finds its explanation in Christ, that the Old Covenant and the New Covenant are one, and not to be separated.

Righteousness, to sum up, has not to be achieved but appropriated.

Questions for further study and discussion on Romans chs. 9.10 —10.8

1. 'Some people do have better spiritual opportunities than others; and of those who have equal opportunities some profit by them others do not. Some nations have received much more gospel light than others—and are correspondingly accountable to God . . .' (F. F. Bruce). Discuss this statement.
2. 'Paul has been misunderstood and unfairly criticized through failure to recognize that it is the God-defying rebel and not the

bewildered seeker after God, whose mouth he so peremptorily shuts' (F. F. Bruce). Consider this statement.

3. 'The Lord knoweth, not only His will, but our heart, in these matters, and where He entirely declines to explain (surely because we are not yet of age to understand Him if He did) He yet shows us Jesus, and bids us meet the silence of the mystery with the silence of a personal trust in the personal Character revealed in Him' (Handley Moule). Ponder this statement.

4.   *'There's a wideness in God's mercy,*
          Like the wideness of the sea;
        There's a kindness in His justice,
          Which is more than liberty.
        But we make His love too narrow
          By false limits of our own;
        And we magnify His strictness
          With a zeal He will not own.'
                  (F. W. Faber)   Do you agree?

5.   ' *"If I ask Him to receive me,*
          Will He say me nay?"
        Not till earth, and not till heaven
          Pass away.'
          (Stephen of Saba)   Is this always true?

6. Are quoted texts sufficient answer in theological discussion today? What of evangelism? How 'far back' must persuasion start in the winning of this generation to Christ?

7. Sum up Israel's mistake.

Romans 10.9–11   The Gospel

The quotation from Deuteronomy contained the words 'mouth' ('lips', RSV) and 'heart'. (Glance at it again.) This suggested a great evangelical verse. 'Mouth' came first in the O.T. quotation, and that would seem to be the only reason for placing confession before belief in the passage before us.

(*i*) *Verse 9.* Observe the content of the confession. The Lordship of Christ, and the resurrection which established and confirmed it, are an integral part, and it is despite to language and history, not only to theology, to call anyone Christian who refuses to accept the fact of the resurrection, not as a philosophical principle or a 'salvation myth', but as an authenticated event (1 Cor. **15.**1–19). Paul nowhere connects the Lordship of Christ with His incarnation only. On the basis of a mutually integrated faith and confession a believer is 'saved'. The death of Christ, and the atonement it signified, is contained in the resurrection, an event impossible without preceding death.

(*ii*) *Verse 10*. The parallelism characteristic of Hebrew is continued, but 'heart' and 'mouth' are now reversed in order. The heart, where the great transaction takes place, means the core of the personality, the true self, stripped of all those accidental accompaniments which may adhere through defect in the body which is the tool of communication; it is the person as God sees it, which shall one day stand before Him. 'Righteousness' is the gift of such faith, and righteousness, thus planted in the 'heart', must permeate the whole person, and 'work itself out' through thought and word and deed.

(*iii*) *Verse 11*. Isa. **28**.16 is quoted. Neither in the Hebrew nor in the Greek version, from which Paul commonly quoted, does the word 'everyone' occur. Paul adds it logically enough, however, and his argument about the universality of salvation turns upon it (see NEB). The verse contains no reference to the Law. He who believes, in the centre of his being, that Christ is Lord, divine and living, and believes it with sincerity and strength enough to avow it—in baptism, in public life, in the face of hostile challenge, in all life's social contexts—is a Christian. No one else is. Nor will such a faith betray him. He will know testing, experience trial, endure pain 'for the name'. If his faith is real, he will never know disillusionment with the One in whom he believed.

Romans 10.12-15   All One in Him

(*i*) *Verses 12 f*. Chapter **3** has already dealt with this truth. The world's vast problems of race find solution here. And consider the tremendous adjustment which the Jew, in Christ, was called upon to make, and which Paul had made. He was not speaking mere theory, beyond the orbit of his personal experience.

Note the natural ease with which Christ is called by the title given to Jehovah (Acts **10**.36; Phil. **2**.10 f.). For the imagery of wealth see Eph. **3**.8. It is a plain fact of common Christian experience, that Christ gives that for which multitudes would pay a price untold—*peace*. The phrase 'calls upon the name of the Lord' (cf. 1 Cor. **1**.2), is a borrowed phrase (Joel **2**.32), but, by the very fact of the lifting of such a text, it is implied that there is no distinction between Christ and God (Acts **9**.14,21; **22**.16; 2 Tim. **2**.22).

(*ii*) *Verse 14*. 'Every one' of v. 13 leads to this digression. 'Every one who calls upon the name of the Lord will be saved'—it therefore follows that the opportunity thus to invoke the name must be put in reach of everyone. It is suggested by A. S. Way in his translation of Paul's letters (a version which should be better known) that Paul frequently set out his letters in abbreviated form. He suggests that the bearer of the letter, who in some cases was the person who took it down from Paul's dictation, would be familiar beforehand with the nature of the communication, and would be sometimes entrusted with supplementary amplification. This suggestion, obviously beyond proof, could account for some of the apparent obscurities in the progress of the argument. This passage is typical. Barclay describes it as 'one of the most difficult and obscure passages in the letter', but if it could be regarded as a set of notes for amplification, rather than a finished communication, much would be explained.

(*iii*) *Verse 15.* Paul's quotation from Isa. **52.**7, produced in his own paraphrase rather than literally, suggests that the closing chapters of the prophecy, which, in their historic context speak of deliverance from exile, were already finding a place in the Christian exegesis of the O.T., as a prophecy of the liberating message of Christ. The interesting point for us is the rapidity with which the O.T. was absorbed into the thinking of the Church.

Meditation: 'No other Name.'

Romans 10.16–21 Israel's Responsibility

(*i*) *Verse 16.* Paul has quoted Isa. **52.** His mind slips to the next chapter in the prophet. His thought moved naturally within the circle of the O.T. The quotation which suggested itself also coincided with an objection which arose from his use of the Isaian oracles as a foreview of the gospel. Will all believe who hear? Is preaching the truth a guarantee of its acceptance? By no means. This, too, is prophesied. John quotes the same passage, no doubt with Paul in mind (**12.**38).

(*ii*) *Verse 17.* The same quotation caused Paul's mind to flash back to the words of v. 14. Here was 'hearing' and the proclaimed word, also in the ancient prophet. It is fascinating to watch his well-stored mind in action.

(*iii*) *Verse 18.* Similarly Paul's mind goes to Psa. **19.**4. Paul refers, of course, to the revelation of God in nature, his earlier theme in the epistle, and the natural theology he developed on different levels in his speech to the Anatolian peasants of Lystra, and to the philosophers of Athen's Areopagus. But Paul may also have had in mind the extent to which the message of Christ had been preached through the synagogues of the Dispersion. His information was complete. Ours is meagre. Were it not for the story of the ministry of Apollos, we should have no inkling of the existence of Christianity in Alexandria. Were it not for the Nazareth Decree, which is reliably dated at about A.D. 49, we would not know that Christianity probably reached Rome in Claudius' day. See Col. 1.6,23.

(iv) *Verse 19.* As for Jewish unbelief, there is the testimony of Moses 'in whom they trusted' (Deut. 32.21). The Church regarded this testimony as extremely significant. Observe Deut. 32.5 reflected in Phil. 2.15; the Septuagint version of Deut. 32.43 (omitted from the Hebrew and most English texts) quoted in Heb. 1.6.

(v) *Verses 20 f.* If this was Moses, Isaiah goes further. Paul ranges his battery of texts against the hostile Jewish opposition with devastating force. The sum of such argument is that, if God has been found and worshipped where conditions seemed so adverse, how inexcusable was Israel for not comprehending their opportunity. The very prophecies should have opened Jewish eyes to the possibility of Israel's supersession. God's arms outstretched (21) were moving testimony in Paul's mind to the tragedy of rejected love, which he, in his final enlightenment, saw historically consummated in Christ.

Romans 11.1–4 The Remnant Again

Chapter 9 stressed that God is sovereign. The next chapter underlined the fact that Israel had sinned. Both themes were pursued with Paul's habitual single-mindedness. In the present chapter he gathers up various matters by-passed in the major drive of his argument. The first is the question: 'Is Israel as a whole rejected?'

Paul first stresses the fact that he, who claims Christ's salvation, he who is the author of the indictment, is himself an Israelite, and has not repudiated his nationhood. He begins with a form of Greek interrogative which suggests a negative answer, and forthwith answers it with vigour. 'I say then, God has not rejected His people, has He? Do not let that thought cross your mind.'

Paul then proceeds to his characteristic O.T. illustration. Read again the story of Elijah in 1 Kings 18,19. The worship of the Phoenician Sun God had flooded the land. Promoted by Jezebel with drive and persecution it seemed supreme. Jezebel was the seal of a trade alliance, and there is no doubt that Ahab's Israel derived immense wealth from business conducted with the busy heathen on the coast. The oil and wheat of Israel, says Ezekiel, went down to Tyre. The wealth of the world flowed back. Ahab was rich. But prosperity is not always good for a nation. With Tyrian goods came Tyrian gods. With Jezebel came Baal. It is possible, therefore, that the choice on Carmel involved more than theology. When the people chose Jehovah they possibly precipitated an economic depression. A break with Jezebel was a break with Tyre.

Swept to decision by Elijah the people nevertheless chose

Jehovah, and streamed home with never a thought of the man who had led them back to God. It broke Elijah. How real, he must have asked, was such a reversal of loyalty? They had cast off Baal. Were they 'truly God's'? After his months of tension, disappointed beyond endurance, and under dire threat, he fled in broken-hearted despair. It was then (1 Kings **19**.18) that the idea of the Remnant was born. Prophecy laid hold of it (Amos **9**.8–10; Mic. **2**.12; **5**.3; Zeph. **3**.12 f.; Jer. **23**.3). Paul saw it operating again.

Romans 11.5, 6 The Chosen

From the thought that the Remnant is the true Israel, two conclusions, consistent with Paul's whole argument, emerge: (*i*) Race alone is not the basis of the choice. If the Remnant who, in prophetic times, and in Paul's own day, represent the 'Israelites indeed' of the Lord's phrase (John **1**.47), it follows that to be a 'Hebrew of the Hebrews' is no final guarantee of God's acceptance. It is of faith in Christ, not the works of the Law. A man is saved, not because his parents were at peace with God, not on the basis of race, family or nation, but because of a personal and individual decision. The principle applied, to their consternation, to the Jews. It applies still. It is curious how the old heresy obtrudes. No church or nation is saved collectively. (*ii*) It also follows that, since the Jews found themselves under the same dispensation of grace as all other peoples, then members of those other races, the Gentiles, could become part of the 'chosen people' by treading the same path to salvation. The notion of a 'chosen people', in fact, has passed through a complete transformation. It is a spiritual idea, not an ethnic one.

Both of these conclusions are, as has been seen in the earlier movement of the argument, consonant with the doctrine which Paul has preached. But in the process he has answered the first question of the chapter. 'Has God cast off His people?' Not at all. A Remnant, as through all time, has accepted Him, and that remnant has become His people, reinforced, as the prophets had also foretold, by additions to their number from the mass of mankind, who found the pathway of faith to Christ's salvation.

Note a final thought emerging from the thought of the 'seven thousand'. Theirs was no aggregate salvation. There was no organism involved, no group-personality, no predetermined number. The seven thousand had not 'bowed the knee to Baal'. Their total was the sum of individual choices, each confessor was a human personality, individually choosing not to submit to the evil which flooded the land.

Paul cannot quench the question which breaks through again. Why, with their manifold advantages, did Israel react like this? He searches the prophets, and disturbing but illuminating oracles rise to his mind. Look at Isa. **6.**9 f.; **29.**10. These were words which haunted the first Jewish Christians, faced with the enormity of their compatriots' apostasy. All four evangelists quote the words (Matt. **13.**14 f.; Mark **4.**12; Luke **8.**10; John **12.**40; Acts **28.**26 f.). Some visitation of God must have caused it. A numbness or a torpor has fallen upon them, not in arbitrary fashion, but as a divine judgement on their rebellion. God has said to them: 'Thy will be done', and as Pharaoh's heart was hardened, so it has tragically befallen those so blessed, so gloriously endowed, who yet persisted in denying the very purpose of their calling and wilfully continued in their sin.

Psa. **69.**22 f. is quoted to similar effect. It was another O.T. passage which came with peculiar force to the early Christians (v. 21, cf. Matt. **27.**48; v. 9, cf. John **2.**17; v. 5, cf. **15.**25). And, again from the same psalm; Paul uses the imagery of blindness recurs in v. 10.

This, however, is not the end of the argument. 'Out of the eater came something to eat', as Samson's riddle had it, and out of Israel's tragedy comes, by God's transforming strength, the salvation of the Gentiles. Then Paul indulges a great hope. What of the glad day when a 'chosen people', Jews and Gentiles combined, the *new* Israel, should stand together 'in Christ'! He is confident that Israel's blindness cannot but be a temporary phenomenon. He was witness of the ingathering of the Gentiles. Then, surely, would come the harvest of the Jews.

A closing word from Handley Moule. The purpose of the quotation from Psa. **69.**22, he says, 'is to enforce the thought that there is such a thing as positive divine action in the self-ruin of the impenitent; a fiat from the throne which "gives" a coma to the soul and beclouds its eyes, and turns its blessings into a curse. Not one word implies the thought that He who so acts meets a soul tending upwards and turns it downwards; that He ignores or rejects even the faintest inquiry after Himself, that He is the author of one particle of the sin of man . . .'

Romans 11.13–16   A Warning to the Gentiles

Almost abruptly Paul turns to the Gentiles among his hearers. It is possible to feel here the first whiff of antisemitism which has left, in some places, and at certain times, a dark stain on the Church.

Were there some in Rome who spoke with contempt of the Jews who had so misconceived their heritage and had done their Messiah to death? Paul himself has just spoken with tenderness and love of his erring people. He has just expressed the lively hope that, in the course of history, Jew and Gentile will be seen together in the fold of Christ. Perhaps he turns to the next phase of his argument because he has at times been conscious of a sense of impatience among his Gentile hearers at the 'stiff-necked' race (13).

Israel's failure, he points out, has been the Gentiles' opportunity. Frequently in Paul's own ministry of the gospel, he had turned to the Gentiles only after the Jews refused to hear him (Acts **13.46-48**; **18.6**; **28.**25–28). And he makes the strange confession that some of the zeal which infused his own ministry was the consciousness that it might 'make his fellow Jews jealous' (14).

Besides, speaking as a devout Jew, he bids his Gentile hearers have respect for history. Alluding to the ritual consecration of the dough in the process of bread-making (Num. **15.**17–21), he points out that the race was one of old renown and ancient dealings with God. They were still, for all their individual rebellion, under the glow of God's past favour. He still remembered the consecration of their beginnings. Or, does the figure imply that the first Christians were Jews, and does Paul suggest that the first-fruits were typical of wider dedication? It is difficult to be dogmatic here in the light of his earlier insistence that the race as a whole had wilfully rebelled. But does not the use of such an argument imply that, whatever the constitution of the Christian community in Rome, it was composed of people uncommonly well taught in the Jewish Scriptures?

The last word to the critical Gentiles reinforces this figure by another: what was the Gentile Christian but a twig, on a tree whose roots ran deep into O.T. history?

Questions and subjects for further study and discussion on Romans chs. 10.9 —11.16

1. What is the significance of confession? Why is it attached to belief?
2. Why *must* the resurrection be part of the Christian message?
3. 'Salvation depends on this: whether a sinful man will make appeal for it to Christ in prayer as to one in whom all God's saving judgement and mercy dwell bodily. It rests with Christ, so appealed to, to make a man partaker in the righteousness of God and eternal life' (James Denney on **10.**12). Comment on this statement in relation to the deity of Christ.
4. How much of the O.T. can be explained only by the N.T?

71

5. Of Paul's quotations from Isaiah and the Psalms in **11**.8–10, Moule writes: 'The context of every citation shows abundantly that those so sentenced are no helpless victims of an adverse fate, but sinners of their own will, in a sense most definite and personal.' Check and discuss.
6. How much does the Christian Church owe to Judaism?

Romans 11.17–21   The Grafted Olive

1. The fact that grafting was believed to rejuvenate a dying olive tree explains the much misunderstood figure which Paul uses here. He speaks of Israel as a dying tree, and of the global Church as a graft upon it. When an olive tree produced badly, a slip of wild olive was grafted, and this was supposed to give new vigour to the tree. Dead branches were lopped and the ancient stock, it was thought, would find expression and new life from and through the engrafted branch, and resume its fruitfulness. Thus, rightly interpreted, Paul's figure becomes a striking picture of Israel and the Church, the succession of the covenants, and the role of Judaism.

This is the best explanation of Paul's figure, true though it may be that the practice is not followed today. Columella, the old soldier of Nero's day, who wrote safe books on agriculture in the days of Nero's Terror, is authority for the practice. It fits the scene exactly.
2. Paul has not lost sight of his warning to the Gentiles against a presumptuous attitude towards those they superseded. The Gentiles are supposed to respond to the imagery of v. 16 with the thought that, far from setting themselves against the root which nourished them, they should think rather of the dead branches stripped by the silviculturist to give them room and space to grow (18 f.). 'Fine,' says Paul ironically ('That is true' [RSV of v. 20] misses the irony). The words of v. 19 are not disputed, but let it be remembered that the arguments and reproaches levelled with some vigour against the Jews in earlier pages of the epistle can be simply reversed. The standing of the Gentiles, as of the Jews, depended on faith, and it is part of a religion which is based on faith in unmerited grace that it excludes all boasting (3.27). The Jews were native branches, proper to the tree, and yet were lopped. Shall not the Gentile graftings be at least as readily pruned?

Thought: Where boasting ends, there dignity can begin.

Romans 11.22–24   The Great Tradition

Paul has felt deeply constrained to frame a warning to the Gentile Christians. The Jews, the world over, had many enemies. Thirty years before Christ was born, Horace, the Roman poet and satirist, had a word of contempt for them. The Book of Esther tells of a threatened pogrom. Alexandria was bitterly divided between Jew and Gentile. There was a real danger, now that Jewry had done its Messiah to death, lest Christians should be tempted to canalize society's dislike of the dispersed race into its own form of hostility and contempt.

Look then, Paul says, at both the kindness and severity of God. The second word picks up the metaphor of v. 17—the 'lopped' branches (RSV 'broken off'). It is a word found nowhere else in the N.T., though, in a couple of contexts, secular Greek writers similarly use it in contrast with 'kindness'. It is *apotomia*, which basically means 'cutting off'. Compare Prov. **29.**1 where the metaphor is as violent—'will suddenly be broken . . .'

How complete is the coverage of the Bible! Paul warned the Gentiles out of his love and agony of mind for his own errant race. And had the Gentiles remembered, the antisemitism which has too often in history found a root in organized Christianity, would have been cut at the root. Hatred for Jews, which marred the medieval Church, would have been replaced by Paul's own yearning and pity, with incalculable results in Jewish evangelism.

There is another aspect of this theme as relevant to the problems of today. The debt of Christianity to the Judaism from which it sprang is part of the figure of the olive tree and the branches, both natural and ingrafted. Nowhere in the N.T. is the O.T. dismissed as irrelevant or disregarded. It is quoted times without number, and it is only a loose attitude towards the authority of the documents of Christianity itself, which is prepared to diminish the authority of the Jewish Scriptures. The Testaments go together and Judaism cannot but be regarded by the Christian as the seed-bed of his own faith. No book in the N.T. better illustrates this than the letter before us.

Romans 11.25–29   Paul's Last Hope

On the strength of a great word from Isaiah (**59.**20 f.) Paul was convinced that the present rebellious attitude of Jewry to the Christian revelation was not final. His mind sought passionately for an explanation of a situation so shocking. True, the Jews were self-willed, and had, of their own act, rejected Christ, but why had God allowed it?

The explanation came to him as a revelation from God. 'I want you,' he said, 'to understand a mystery.' The word 'mystery' occurs once only in the Gospels (Mark **4.**11 and the parallel passages in Matthew and Luke); John never uses the word, but Paul uses it twenty-two times. It is used (i) to describe the Christian revelation as a whole (Rom. **16**.25; Eph. **1**.9; Col. **2**.2); (ii) to describe some special aspect of the Christian revelation (Eph. **3**.3; 1 Cor. **15**.51; and the present passage). Paul claims, in a word, that God had revealed to him that the Jews had been, of God's set purpose, permitted to go their self-willed way, in order to clear the ground for the surge of the Gentiles into the Church. At a certain point, he was sure, this would stir the Jews to divine jealousy, so that they would return to the Lord.

Enormous difficulties gather round Paul's prediction: 'all Israel shall be saved'. Perhaps this is one of the passages which illustrate A. S. Way's theory of abbreviation. Perhaps the bearer of the letter was entrusted with supplementary explanation. On the face of it 'all Israel' means all Israelites, and leaves it unstated whether that universal expression means all Israelites through all their history, or all Israelites alive at some historic moment of illumination and reconciliation. If Paul meant this he contradicted his doctrine of salvation by faith, which is the deep contention of this epistle. He has claimed, however, a special revelation from God, and therefore he could not thus contradict himself.

Difficult though the interpretation is on the face of the words, Paul must have meant the 'new Israel', the sum total of the redeemed. This is the one interpretation which conserves his consistency, safeguards his authority, and preserves the argument from the incongruous conclusion that Israel is, after all, not responsible, is a specially favoured people, and will be perforce all saved. This interpretation must be hazarded if the doctrine of the whole epistle is to hold together. Commentators, of course, who diminish Paul's inspiration and authority, dismiss the argument as emotional, and accuse the apostle of trying 'to have it both ways' (e.g. C. H. Dodd, p. 182). Let v. 26 but be regarded as a reference to a Spiritual Israel, and the pattern of argument works neatly to a conclusion.

Romans 11.30–36 The Poetry of Faith

It is with some relaxation of the mind that the reader turns to the closing verses, the epilogue of this powerful and difficult chapter. As Wm. Barclay says: 'Here theology turns to poetry. Here the seeking of the mind turns to the adoration of the heart.'

At any rate, God's last purpose for mankind has been set powerfully forth. He designs mercy for Jew and Gentile alike. Man's rebellion itself is to subserve the vast plan, for it has been shown that God has permitted all men, Jews and Gentiles, to fall into a common disobedience, in order that both, reduced to a common humility

74

and conviction of sin, may turn in penitence to the acceptance of His grace (32).

We need not linger over the meaning of 'mercy upon all'. Paul has been accused of universalism at this point, but that reproach would again involve him in self-contradiction. His words mean no more than that God's mercy is equally available to all. It is thrust on no Pharaoh (F. F. Bruce has a lucid note on the various meanings of 'universalism' in the *Tyndale N.T. Commentary, p.* 223).

The truth more properly considered here is the fact, demonstrated in man's spiritual experience, that no situation is beyond the transforming power of God. In our personal lives, it is found true that anything, good or evil, triumph or disaster, success or failure, loss or gain, all things, committed in utter faith to God, can be transmuted into blessing. This is one of the basic truths of Calvary. And what is experimentally true in personal experience, is also true in the wider context of universal history. In this we begin to gain a glimpse of a final consummation in which sin, the fall, pain, and all the haunting inexplicable realities, all the burden of what Wordsworth called 'this unintelligible world', will be at last drawn into a final superbly satisfying pattern of blessing. And so the God who directs, also permits, and in the end commands all things to serve Him. But how important it is for the modern mind to think of both a directive and a permissive will, if God, in the context of such Providence, is to be rightly understood. For consolation in concluding the study of these difficult chapters turn to Peter's remark—2 Pet. **3.**15 f.

Romans 12.1–2   The Application

Paul is always determined that conduct should not be lost in doctrine. He would have agreed with one of his perceptive commentators, F. B. Meyer, who said: 'Some weave a veil of doctrine which screens the Saviour from their eyes. It is emblazoned with creeds, definitions and orthodox statements of truth. It is not Christ, but doctrines about Christ which inspire them. The death of Christ rather than the Christ who died; the resurrection rather than the risen One; the priesthood rather than the Priest. The correctness of our notions about the Saviour may even cause us to miss the Saviour Himself.'

Verse 1. Paul has already touched on this obligation (**6.**12 f.). A faith which does not penetrate and enliven the activities of the body in all its actions and common tasks, was not in Paul's view a faith at all. It is a pity that the RSV did not abandon the word 'holy' (note NEB, 'dedicated'). The word has become discoloured in common use. Its basic meaning in Greek seems to be 'set apart for divine use'. The person of the Christian is 'consecrated' to God, and this, the verse concludes, is the purpose for which he was created and redeemed. 'Our heart cannot be quieted,' said Augustine, 'till it find repose in God.'

Verse 2. Here is a literal translation: 'And cease trying to adapt yourself to the age we live in, but continue the transformation which began with your mind's renewal, so that you may test out for yourselves the will of God, that, namely, which is good, well-pleasing to Him, and perfect.'

A crowded sentence of the sort Paul often wrote. He is eager to thrust home the truth that surrender to Christ involves rebirth, the passage from death to life. The two present tenses have been emphasized in the translation to bring out the fact that the Christian's life is not a sudden and miraculous metamorphosis, but a process aided and forwarded by the active and dedicated will. Two Greek voices merge in the two imperatives. 'Be transformed' (passive) and 'transform yourselves' (middle) are the same word. There is no need to choose one rendering and exclude the other. They blend, and in the blending underline a truth, the blessed fact that God promotes our transformation, but in active partnership with the Christian. Thus we 'work out our own salvation' (Phil. **2.**12).

'The age we live in . . .' Paul was writing to Christians in Rome which shared Corinth's reputation for evil. There is a strong urge in everyone to 'do at Rome as Rome does', but the Christian must guard his response. He must never conform to the vice, the evil, the 'permissiveness' of a godless society.

Romans 12.3–5   The Body of Christ

Verse 3. The RSV misses the point in the concluding phrase. Let us translate the latter half of the verse thus: '. . . but to cultivate a balanced soundness of mind, according as God has given to every man faith as a measure.'

There is no suggestion that God metes out a varied capacity for faith. Faith may be had for the asking, and, like God's Spirit in John's phrase (**3.**34), is not 'given out of a measure'. Faith *is* the measure, the measuring instrument (Rev. **21.**15), by which a man can assess his Christian balance, and soundness of mind. According to a man's faith, so will a man judge himself, his attitudes, testimony, and vocation. No other rendering makes sense.

Verse 4. The metaphor of the body is developed in 1 Cor. **12**, and appears again in Col. **1.**18 and Eph. **4.**15 f. The idea is found in Plato, another indication of Paul's wide reading, and may reflect conversations with Luke, the physician. The body is healthy when all its parts co-operate, each in its proper sphere. The less visible parts, as pathology demonstrates, are as vital to full health, indeed, to life, as the more visible parts. Microscopic malfunctions produce tragic diseases. So with the Church.

Verse 5. For the sake of each, and for the sake of all, it behoves us to find, by that judgement and discernment which faith can temper and control (3), the proper function allotted to us, to perform that function with zest and smooth efficiency, and not to hanker for a role and place for which we were not shaped and intended. The dependence of all is upon Christ.

'Balanced soundness of mind' is the key to such correctness of Christian conduct. It is reason, sanctified by the indwelling Christ, and co-operating with faith, which shapes the awareness of the part we are to play and helps us to play it well with no thought of envy or regret. We are equally significant. The widow of Zarephath, the child with loaves and fish, Simon of Cyrene, and the woman at the Treasury, did not realize how important was the part each played.

And note that it is equally damaging for a healthy member of the body to remain inactive, as for any member to usurp a role for which nature did not design it. Both faults cripple the body of Christ.

Romans 12.6–8 Functions Vary

Verse 6. Prophecy is that informed exposition of Christian truth which was of prime importance in the Church before the N.T. was rounded and complete. Prophecy differed from teaching by its possessing a peculiar and historically transient sense of functioning under guidance and inspiration. It consequently needed control by reason and by faith. A balanced faith could preserve a man with 'prophetic' gifts from the temptation to exaggerate or distort. Let the 'prophet', Paul says, deliver the full truth as his apprehension of Christ provides the insight. Let him keep his faith strong and whole, his personal committal to Christ complete, and in such humble integrity speak out. So he will edify.

Verse 7. 'If our gift be service, let us exercise it in its proper sphere, and likewise if our gift be teaching.' This translation leaves open, as the Greek word allows, the question which has bothered some translators (Weymouth, Moffatt, NEB, Goodspeed), whether such service is given within the sphere of the Christian community, or in society at large. Within the Church the tasks which confront those called to serve (and who is not?) are multitudinous. Problems of family, housing, the aged, the difficulties of mothers, widows, orphans, the lonely, the sick, the poor, and other tasks of mutual aid, are too often neglected because too many fail to take seriously a call to a Christian function in practical service.

And what of teaching? Neglect of thought and study is a widespread source of weakness. No ministry prospers which neglects the teaching function. A well-taught congregation is a stable community. Teaching, too, functions on many levels. It demands much and too few pay the price.

Verse 8. 'Exhortation' flows from an ardent personality. It is something added to prophecy and teaching. But it must be natural, not forced. Unerringly Paul touches the fault which haunts each virtue. Let the rich be liberal, but without ulterior motives. 'Let the leader lead with zeal', runs the third phrase, never asking his followers to do what he hesitates to do himself. Let the man of mercy not spoil his ministration with mournfulness or artificial heartiness.

Observe how 'balanced soundness of mind' keeps every virtue and activity sweet. Each 'gift' can be spoiled by its own inherent exaggeration, or the spoiling infusion of self.

Questions and subjects for further study and discussion on Romans chs. 11.7—12.8

1. Name three ways in which the O.T. foreshadowed the N.T., and in which Judaism prepared the way for Christianity.
2. In what way does the Epistle to the Romans stress the debt of the Church to Judaism?
3. 'Theology is doxology or it is nothing at all' (E. Stauffer). Consider this.
4. Consider such words as 'holy', 'saint', 'saved' in the vocabulary of evangelism.
5. What disciplines aid the Christian's transformation?
6. List the 'gifts', of all sorts, necessary to the smooth and harmonious functioning of your church.

Romans 12.9–13   The Christian's Graces

Verse 9. The second and third precepts go closely with the first. True Christian love depends upon a genuine appreciation of spiritual values. In utter sincerity, it neither condones evil nor overlooks good. To 'hate that which is evil' without 'holding fast to that which is good' produces a self-righteous, censorious attitude. The reverse process produces the sentimentalist, soft, emotional, indulgent. Christian love avoids both extremes.

Verse 10. The 'honour' mentioned relates to the respect paid to

each other by members of a cultivated society. Paul refers to this
social grace in 13.7. The two precepts balance. Brotherly love is
not intended to produce a deadening egalitarianism, in which rank
is unrecognized and worth unhonoured. Rank and status, in such a
society, breeds no self-esteem, and begets no servility. An eagerness
in each to recognize another's worth is a surer road to communal
happiness and easy fellowship than a plebeian jealousy of all who
stand out from the mass.

Verse 11. The word translated 'zeal' occurs twelve times in the
N.T., and is translated in the RSV and AV(KJV) in seven ways,
ranging from 'haste' to 'care'. It conveys the idea of earnestness
and keenness. To hold such an attitude a Christian must be ardent
and dedicated. Apollos is the model (Acts 18.25).

Verse 12. The RSV incorrectly inserts 'your'. The three commands
are related. Paul was no pessimist. Hope receives his blessing. Had
any man a braver hope than he, who aimed to conquer an Empire
for his Lord? True hope is not tense and anxious. It can only rightly
claim the name when it produces patience in time of stress. And
patience sustains itself by steadfast prayer. Christian optimism is
no wilful blindness to grim facts. The dark side of life must be
faced, but from facing it comes discipline in prayer, and waiting on
God.

Verse 13. Note again Paul's striving for balanced conduct. Paul
begs the Roman Christians, some of them slaves, to bear each other's
needs. But he wants no closed and introverted society. The word
'hospitality' means literally 'love of strangers'. A Christian closing
of the ranks can be forbidding to 'the outsider'. The corrective is
an open heart to the world at large. 'Pursue hospitality', he says,
implying active search for opportunity in this matter of outreaching
friendliness. The verb is rendered variously as 'pursue', 'aim', and
'seek' in 9.30 f.; 14.19; 1 Cor. 14.1; 1 Thess. 5.15.

Romans 12.14–17   The Virtue of Understanding

Verse 14. The curse referred to is the formal commination, an
Eastern practice. Psa. 137, for example, envisages a harassed group,
meeting, as Jews did when in exile, by the river (Acts 16.13), and
menaced by a hostile Babylonian crowd. Hence the too frequently
misunderstood maledictions of the closing verses. The small,
threatened group may have saved their lives by the act of invoking
upon their foes the evil their foes had inflicted on them. The psalm
is a cameo drama, and is not to be judged out of context. The precept
forbids the Christian such forms of self-defence.

Verse 15. To laugh with the gay is easy. To weep in true fellowship with the distressed puts a stronger strain upon love and sincerity (John **11**.35 f.). Pity is best taught by fellowship in trouble, and pity is a Christlike virtue. And nothing but Christ's pity suffices for the tragedy of self-tormented man.

Verse 16. The Christlike sympathy of the last verse calls for understanding, and understanding is never found in the self-centred, because it grows from the habit of considering another's point of view. Wand translates: 'Try and share in the common thoughts and aspirations of the rest.' Paul is asking for the 'like-mindedness' he commended to the Philippians (**2**.2; **4**.2). Personal ambition and place-seeking wreck such fellowship. Hence the second precept. There must, of course, be leadership, and Paul set some in charge of the churches he founded. Nor were they to be denied respect and deference. But that is not to promote the active quest for dignity and office in those not called to it. True eminence, however, is not self-conscious. It moves easily among all ranks. The fourth precept sums up the verse: 'Avoid conceit.' The N.T. condemns self-esteem uncompromisingly. Conceit is the child of pride, and pride is a fundamental sin.

Verse 17. 'Return no man evil for evil. Practise good before all men.' The precepts follow naturally. Paul suggests by the verb he uses that the return blow might well have been deserved. But a policy of 'tit for tat' is not Christian. Moreover, there is no time or occasion for such petty vengefulness if the preoccupation of the life is the active doing of good. Consider 1 Cor. **13**. 'Conceit may puff a man up,' said Ruskin, 'but can never prop him up.'

Romans 12.18–21   The Way to Treat Enemies

Verse 18. 'All' again ends the verse, and it is moving to remember that Paul addressed his letter to a church which numbered imperial slaves among its members. It was difficult for those who lay under the burden of servitude and its vast injustice not to harbour resentment, and resentment so often issues in acts of hostility. Live at peace, Paul says, 'as far as you can', recognizing that strife is sometimes not of the victim's own making.

Verse 19. 'Leave room for God's wrath,' says Paul. Let the wronged do nothing, only stand out of the way. God needs a clear field, uncluttered by human efforts, to accelerate the working of the moral law. 'Be still before the Lord, and wait patiently for Him' (Psa. **37**.7). Serenity is healthy, elusive though it may be. It dwells within, and not in circumstances. The key to it is a submissive will. Petrarch listed five foes to peace—anger, ambition, avarice, envy and pride. Paul has dealt with them all. Read Isa. **20** and then the closing verses of Isa. **54**.

Verse 20. Beware, none the less, of a passive attitude. Paul bids his Romans not only abstain from active retaliation, but to seek to do good to those who harm them. This, in fact, could have been an effective form of evangelism. The last words are frequently misquoted. They come from Prov. **25.**21 f., and speak of the pain of shame and self-reproach, which engender conviction of sin and a search for salvation. To see kindness to the undeserving and the hostile as a subtle form of vengeance is not to take Paul correctly. He regards such goodness as a testimony, and a mode of Christian witness.

Verse 21. The last words sum up the chapter. Paul wants no ethical vacuum. He wants constructive activity. Evil can never overcome evil. Two wrongs have never made a right. Evils only breed and perpetuate their kind. Good, on the other hand, neutralizes and replaces.

Here, then, is Christian character. Such are the men and women whom grace would make. Such is salvation in action. Salvation means quiet of mind and heart, purpose that consumes each day's reborn energy, the recovery of significance, a happiness which finds meaning in all experience, the 'abundant life' of Christ's promise (John **10.**10). 'Something lives,' as the hymn says, 'in every hue Christless eyes have never seen.' As Francis Thompson stated:

> ' *'Tis ye, 'tis your estrangéd faces,*
> *That miss the many-splendoured thing . . .'*

Romans 13.1–5 Christian Citizenship

It is important to see Christian society in the first century in proper perspective. The Empire, running to the Rhine, the Danube, and the Black Sea, and bounded to the west by the Atlantic, and to the south and east by the great deserts, had given the Mediterranean world a stable peace. The Roman Peace was the social and political framework within which the Christian Church attained its first international form.

Roman history, written from the standpoint of the aristocratic writers of the capital, inevitably concentrated on Rome itself, on the vices and doings of the court and the prince, ignoring the proletariat, and the provinces. It is historic fact that, during the principate of the youthful Nero, whose vice and profligacy became legendary, the provinces enjoyed such quietness and stability that 'Nero's Five Years', the quinquennium during which government was largely controlled by the wise Seneca, and the soldierly Burrus, became a legend of just administration throughout the Roman world.

Paul had learned in Gallio's court, and he was to learn again in riotous Jerusalem, that Roman discipline and justice, rough though it sometimes was, and corrupt though it could be in such vicious hands as those of Felix, was a protection and a shield. Moreover, the Jews were restive throughout the world. The mood of the Empire's most difficult people was heating towards the tragic explosion of A.D. 66, and that event had world-wide repercussions. As Paul found when seeking a passage from Corinth to Jerusalem, and again in Jerusalem itself, a collaborating Jew such as he was, with his assumption of Roman citizenship, was in acute danger.

He was also hopeful that the fabric of the Empire could be Christianized, and he did not wish the Church to become branded as a dissident, rebellious group. A decade later Rome drove the Church into this position, but hope of partnership still lived when Paul was writing. The Empire, too, was sensitive about organizations within its body. Hence these wise words, repeated in 1 Tim. 2.1 f. and Tit. 3.1, and echoed in 1 Pet. 3.13–17.

Paul's own growing awareness of the power and usefulness of the Empire in his programme of evangelism may be traced in Acts. It takes first form in Cyprus, reached a climax in Philippi, and may be illustrated from Corinth, Ephesus and Jerusalem.

Romans 13.6–10   Debt of Love

The taxes levied by both imperial and local government were manifold, but generally administered and collected with greater justice under the Empire than under the earlier Republic. But whatever they were, taxes were an obligation, and it is a practical application of Paul's previous exhortation to obedient citizenship that all obligations should be met.

Christian tradition was firmly established long before the four Gospels were written. More than once Paul speaks of having handed on 'what he had received' (1 Cor. 11.23; 15.3). There was a corpus of apostolic information, carefully conserved and diligently transmitted. Mark's Gospel is the written account of what Peter gave his young convert. In this chapter it is possible to watch Paul's mind ranging over the account received, and recalling the memorable reply concerning the tribute money (Matt. 22.21).

The recollection takes his mind on to the incident recorded in Matt. 22.35–40, and he echoes the tradition yet to be recorded. Perhaps he also remembers the story of the rich youth, who professed to have kept all the commandments, for the order in which the commandments are listed reflects Luke **18**.20, and not the Exod. **20** order. It is interesting to see his thought moving over a firm, clear body of tradition. So remote was the Church from the practice alleged by one strange school of literary criticism, which imagines it reading back into the saga of Christ incidents which they created to justify practice, belief or emerging forms of worship.

There is a debt of love which each man owes to all mankind. If a man honestly endeavours to discharge this debt, he will naturally not harm his neighbour, so needs no prohibitions to hedge his path. Sexual sin, for all the vapid romanticizing which surrounds it, results not from love, but from too little love, from selfishness and introverted carnality. Love never destroys, so does not harm another's life, never deprives and so inhibits stealing. Love rejoices in another's advantage, and so does not covet. This was the closing theme of the N.T., the First Epistle of John. It was the preoccupation of the last of the apostles, that which he finally and most vividly remembered of the One with whom he had walked sixty years before.

Romans 13.11–14 Clothed in Christ

Verse 11. No difficulty should be felt in the apostle's expectation of Christ's coming. How could it be otherwise? We know nothing of the future, and the N.T. gives no clue to the date of history's consummation, save that it follows an age of mounting sin and accelerating apostasy. What of today? And for the first time, faced by the accumulating heritage of human sin and folly, the scientists have become frequent prophets of doom.

Verse 12. The 'works of darkness' are deeds which shun the light of day, and therefore are not Christian (John **3**.20 f.). The Christian's life is not a sleep but a battle. For 'the armour of light' see the full development of the image in Eph. **6**.

Verse 13. Note the vices which Paul chooses to stress. Revelling is the unbecoming noise of the drunken and the selfish, the creation of disturbance common enough in the overcrowded environment of today's urban civilization, as it was in Paul's similarly city-ridden world. The Christian should conduct himself with dignity, quietness and thought for the tranquillity of others. Drunkenness is disgusting folly in anyone. The Christian should properly boycott alcohol, if he is to follow with any care Paul's argument in 1 Cor. **8**. Alcoholism claims from five to ten per cent of social drinkers, causes crime untold, and accidents without number. A Christian can argue for 'moderate drinking' on no grounds of sincerity. The third vice was immorality, the 'debauchery' of the odd rendering in the RSV. It has taken the world nineteen centuries to return to the 'permissiveness' of Rome's society. Chastity was scorned. It is scorned again. The fourth word is 'shamelessness'; 'licentiousness' is not a good translation. The stage has begun, for the first time since the scandalous nude theatre of Nero's day, to dare thus to flout virtue. It is uncanny how this decade has turned many a wheel full circle. 'Contention' or 'quarrelling' is the opposite of love. It is based on self-assertion. 'Jealousy' is similarly love's negation, for it thrives on self-esteem.

Verse 14. This is the famous verse of Augustine's conversion. He tells of it in his *Confessions* (8-end). The metaphor is that of clothing oneself in the moral disposition and character of Christ, taking not the armour of the earlier figure (as in the NEB) but rather garments which, after all, are the most visible feature of us. Phillips gets it well: 'Let us be Christ's men from head to foot, and give no chances to the flesh to have its fling.'

Romans 14.1–6 The Weaker Brother

The sudden raising of the matter of 'the man who is weak in faith' is a little puzzling. The unemancipated Christian was a common problem. In Colossae, in the Lycus valley, the legalism which was a mark of the type Paul has in mind, had attached itself to strange doctrines and elaborate superstitions, and called down the apostle's vigorous denunciation. In Galatia the deviant Christians had cluttered their faith with elements from a discarded Judaism. In Rome, as in Corinth, the group whose inadequacies Paul recognized, seem not to have been coherent or powerful. They are 'weaker brethren', and are not addressed directly. They are mentioned because they constitute a real problem for the Christian community.

We have already quoted 1 Cor. **8**. In the course of the argument of that epistle, Paul saw that his own liberty was curtailed in love because its full exercise might cause misunderstanding among those who did not share his insight into the meaning of the freedom he had found in Christ. Likewise here. He bids the community at large not argue with 'the weak in faith', but receive him, presumably in the spirit of Christian love and understanding, which has been a theme of the last two chapters. The weak, in such fellowship, could become strong.

Who were these 'weaklings'? We have suggested that the Roman church was a mixed body. There would be Jews who had recognized Christ, and with them Gentile proselytes, who had first turned to Judaism from the vice and paganism of their world, and then had moved on to Christ. Thirdly, there would be Gentile converts who had come to Christ directly. It may, indeed, have been difficult for converted Jews and proselytes to grasp in full significance that it was all of faith. No prohibitions and taboos based on law and regulation now existed. It was now a matter of faith, and after that of love. It was a weakness of faith not so to move to freedom. Hence the phrase.

Romans 14.7–12 'No Man is an Island'

As so often happens in the writings of great souls, the particular turns to universal truth. Distilled from the words doubtless directed towards a special problem reported from Rome comes this great passage which touches the very heart of our humanity, and our deep responsibility. It is a fact that we are part of a body. This is one of the slender threads which bind this chapter, and this penetrating utterance to what went before in the letter. Phillips renders: 'The truth is that we neither live nor die as self-contained units. At every turn life links us to the Lord, and when we die we come face to face with Him' (7 f.).

The translator perhaps had in mind a word of the Dean of St. Paul's, three and a half centuries old. 'No man is an Island,' wrote John Donne, 'entire of itself. Every man is a piece of the Continent, a part of the Main . . . Any man's death diminishes me, because I am involved in Mankind. And therefore never send to know for whom the bell tolls. It tolls for thee.' Thomas Hughes, author of the Victorian classic *Tom Brown's Schooldays*, wrote of Arnold, Rugby's historic headmaster: 'He taught us that, in this wonderful world, no boy can tell which of his actions is indifferent and which not. He taught us that, by a thoughtless word or look, we may lead astray a brother for whom Christ died. He taught us that a boy's only safety and only wisdom lies in bringing the whole life into obedience to Him who made us for Himself and redeemed us with His own precious blood.' Such, too, is the theme of the Bible: '. . . she took of its fruit and ate; and she also gave some to her husband, and he ate' (Gen. **3**.6). And see again 1 Cor. **8**.13; **9**.12, and most solemn of all, Isa. **53**.6. Christ was 'involved in mankind'. The Christian hermit, trying to escape such involvement, like the pagan Epicurean before him, betrays a trust.

For this we shall give account. Consider vs. 10,12. There will be a time and place where we shall face ourselves and God, where every word and action shall be seen undistorted and in its true light. We shall one day stand in the full blaze of truth, and that overwhelming fact should be part always of our thinking. In the light of it who are we to judge our brother, we who know so little of ourselves, let alone the perplexities of another? It is only 'the gold, silver, the precious stones' which we have built upon the foundation of our salvation which will survive that Scrutiny.

'Then, O my Lord, prepare my soul for that great day.'

Questions and subjects for further study and discussion on Romans chs. 12.9—14.12
1. Distinguish love from indulgence.
2. Assess the part of hospitality in winning others.
3. Why is pride a vice?
4. What guidance may the modern Christian find in Paul's attitude towards constituted civil authority?
5. How can a Christian have rules without being legalistic?
6. Should Christians ever argue over 'scruples', or is each Christian sovereign in such matters?
7. What is conscience? Is it a sure guide?

Romans 14.13–23   Our Debt of Tolerance

'We owe the world,' says an Arab proverb, 'a debt of tolerance.' Paul's continued insistence on this issue seems to indicate that he is answering a specific enquiry. In both the letters to Corinth and to Philippi there is indication that replies are being made to queries and comments sent to him. We should understand what he writes better if the letters written to him had been also preserved.

The point he makes, with some urgency, is that even when a person is right in a certain view, his conviction must not be thrust upon others without regard to their feelings. There are ways of persuasion, and gentleness is not compromise. This is not to be taken as an excuse for blurred thinking on matters of moral and ethical importance, nor to suggest that it is wrong to hold the firmest of convictions. Paul only pleads for discernment over what is vital and what is not, and for the tolerance which respects another's earnest scruples.

The reference to a 'stumbling-block' in v. 13 (cf. v. 21) reveals how deep this problem goes, and at the same time Paul's spiritual insight. Suppose the example of the 'emancipated' Christian, a powerful personality perhaps, leads a weaker man to adopt a practice which his conscience condemns? The man who so acts has suffered damage. An occasion for stumbling has been put in his path. Paul knew what Christ had said on moral defilement; it is not in things but in the heart (Mark 7.20–23). (Here is another indication of the reality of the oral tradition.) He is not in any sense superseding the Lord's words but applying them in the Lord's name to a special situation. Vv. 14 and 15 continue v. 13. Align, too, v. 17 with Matt. **5.**6,9 f., 12 and **6.**31. It is again fairly clear that Christ's words were the common currency of Christian thought, either from records antedating the present Gospels, or from the oral tradition.

In the light of this challenging statement on Christian responsibility what would the Christian answer be to Cain's surly question: 'Am I my brother's keeper?'? It is a question to be answered before the judgement seat (10).

Romans 15.1–13 One in Christ

In this section we cover thirteen verses. They deal, in the main, with truths and counsel underlined earlier in the letter. As we read through the letter, and draw near to the mind and heart of the writer, it is possible in these two concluding chapters to sense his relaxed mood. A tense and difficult theological exposition is ended. He has written chapter after chapter of vigorous and fervent reasoning which has engaged all his powers. It was doubtless a relief to turn to simpler, if not unimportant questions, the peace of the church, its principles of fellowship, and finally the personal greetings which always closed an ancient letter.

With the notion of the Christian community as a functioning body still in his mind, Paul begs the Roman Christians to help one another. Phillips renders v. 1 in a homely but effective way: 'We who have strong faith ought to shoulder the burden of the doubts and qualms of others and not just to go our own sweet way.' A church should be marked by mutual understanding and concern. Such is the spirit of Christ (3).

Harmony was the apostle's deep concern. The plea for harmony dictated the Philippian letter. He pleads for it here, and shows that it grows round Christ. Those actively at one with Him are naturally at one with each other (5). So is God honoured before men (6). Disharmony shatters testimony.

The next two verses hint at a source of possible division. We have seen that a rift between the attitudes of Jewish and Gentile Christians could have been the occasion of the impatience deprecated in the last chapter. With some delicacy Paul now hints to the Jews that the Gentiles, who had joined them in the Christian community, merited a welcome (8). Indeed they were a fulfilment of prophecy (8–12; Psa. **18.**49; Deut. **32.**43; Psa. **117.**1; Isa. **11.**10).

From the last quotation, anxious not to press his point, but to allow the ancient Scriptures to carry their own persuasion to the minds of those who revered them, he picked up the word 'hope' and bracketed a verse with it (13). It is quite exquisitely tactful, and is not, as Hilaire Belloc said, 'the grace of God in courtesy'?

Romans 15.14–21 Apostle to the Gentiles

It is often assumed, perhaps because of the altercation with Barnabas over Mark (Acts 15.39), or because of his bold confrontation of Peter (Gal. 2.11), that Paul was a stern man, intense and rigid. The impression is quite wrong. The last note ended with a reference to courtesy. Paul was indeed courteous, loving, gentle and tactful. He wrote the letter to Philippi because he felt in conscience bound to rebuke two women dissidents. He spent three chapters speaking of unity, exalting Christ, and gently exhorting the church, and only then did he mention Euodia and Syntyche, quickly following the needed rebuke with words of commendation.

The Roman church clearly needed the most careful instruction in matters vital to the Christian faith. Its Jewish element in particular required a deeper appreciation of the role and the limitations of Judaism. It is also clear that the place of the Gentiles was not secure. Paul has discharged his duty of instruction, and discharged it faithfully. He now turns with warmth and cordiality to comfort those who may have found his uncompromising doctrine daunting, and failed to see the compassion and concern with which he spoke to them.

He reminds them, too, of his God-given office. He was the apostle to the Gentiles, and purposed soon to preach in the capital of the Empire. He had long worked to that end. In a great arc of territory from Antioch of Syria and Cyprus to Illyricum, at the western end of the Egnatian Way, he had sought to plant his Christian cells in the chief cities of the Mediterranean world—Antioch of Pisidia, bastion of Roman power in central Asia Minor, Ephesus, the great religious centre and proconsular seat, Philippi, strategic key to northern Greece, Corinth, crossroads of central Mediterranean trade, Athens, intellectual capital of the world—and Rome remained. The sheer scope of such evangelism is overwhelming. Set it beside our feeble exploitation of the vast facilities for communication at the Church's disposal today, and let us pray, even as Christ commanded, that more reapers be sent forth into the ready harvest. And who, if not those who pray?

The passage is poignantly autobiographical. In pursuance of his audacious plan of winning the Empire to Christ, Paul had set Spain in his programme of evangelism. It was a sure instinct. Spain gave Rome much. The bulk of the meagre remains of Latin literature which have survived from the fifties and the sixties of the first century was the work of Spaniards. Seneca, Nero's tutor and prime minister, his nephew Lucan, the epic poet, and several others prominent in Rome's contemporary cultural life, came from Spain. Spain was also to provide three emperors, including Trajan and Hadrian.

Whether Paul ever did reach the great western peninsula we do not know. If he did not, the plan was wrecked by his visit to Jerusalem. In Jerusalem the intransigent Pharisaic wing of the Christian Church was domiciled. Paul, who had been a Pharisee, yearned to win them. He knew that they looked askance at his Gentile evangelism, and his scheme was to demonstrate Gentile love by carrying to Jerusalem a large sum of money, contributed by the Christians of the Empire, to relieve poverty in the Jerusalem community.

The poverty was no doubt real, and may have come about to some extent because of the short-lived experiments in Christian communism recorded in the early chapters of Acts. Jerusalem was tense amid the growing terrorism of the countryside, and the deepening opposition to Roman rule. The Empire sought to hold the turbulent province with a meagre garrison of 3,000, based at Caesarea. Procuratorial government was weak and inadequately armed. Paul knew that he risked his life (30,32). He persisted in his project, as Luke frankly narrates, against all advice. He failed to win the dissidents. The journey led to his arrest and imprisonment. God overruled and brought him none the less to Rome. Precious documents of the N.T., the 'prison epistles', no less than Luke's two books, for which the research was done while Paul was in protective custody at Caesarea, arose from what, on the face of it, was a catastrophe. Read the story and assess Paul's mood, his expectations, and his disapprovement, in Acts **21—23**.

Romans 16.1–6   Greetings and Commendations

Such chapters are of more interest than might at first be thought. These verses introduce some of the personalities of the early Church, give some insight into its social structure, and reveal with what habitual facility people moved about through the Mediterranean world. People today may move in such lands with greater speed. They could hardly move with less impediment.

Phoebe was a 'deaconess' of Corinth, a rich woman probably, who lived on the seaboard of Corinth's eastern port. If deaconess is not too technical a term, Phoebe was the first on record to hold the office. Paul may have written the letter in her home, and she may have undertaken to carry it to Rome.

Prisca, or more familiarly, Priscilla, and her husband Aquila, were a much travelled pair. They were also Paul's hosts at Corinth. They had been expelled from Rome in A.D. 49 when Claudius legislated against the Jews, and opened a cloth or tent-making business in Corinth (Acts **18.**2,18,24–26; 1 Cor. **16.**19; 2 Tim. **4.**19). The references show that this earnest couple fostered churches both in Corinth and Ephesus. Now they are back in Rome. Aquila had come from Pontus. They illustrate the home-based nature of the early Church (Philem. 2), and also the vital nature of a joint testimony by a husband and wife of like mind.

Since Aquila and Priscilla were last heard of in Ephesus, the bold suggestion has been made that this chapter was a letter, or part of a letter to Ephesus which somehow became attached to the epistle to Rome. The suggestion is typical of the nonsense which sometimes invades N.T. studies. The only basis for such a theory is someone's inability to accept the mobility of ancient populations. There is no evidence to support it. Irresponsible conjecture, rashly rushed into print, has been for a century a feature of Biblical studies which would not be tolerated in any other branch of literary criticism and exegesis.

But to conclude on a more constructive note: again we see a feature of the first century which marks the twentieth—habits of travel, immigration and change of residence, all of which propagated and spread the gospel. Can this be harnessed again?

Romans 16.7–16 Honours Roll

Twenty-six Christians in Rome are mentioned by name in this chapter, several of them women. Observe the affection and generosity of Paul's reference to them. Some had known Christ before he did. Others had shared his imprisonment. Thirteen of the names occur in documents or inscriptions relating to Caesar's vast community of slaves, freedmen and clients. These names, of course, are not uncommon, and the reference may not be to the same individuals. Paul, however, does speak in Phil. **4.**22 of Christians in Caesar's household, and in v. 11 he refers to Christians in the household of Narcissus, the notorious freedman of Claudius. His household was a coherent whole, although Nero had killed him two or three years earlier. It is likely that Aristobulus was the grandson of Herod the Great. Claudius, who, in his foreign policy, imitated Augustus, had close relations with the Herodian house, and it is known that Aristobulus was educated in Rome. His household may have been absorbed into that of Claudius at Aristobulus' death, but would retain a distinctive identity. It is evident that the imperial household was deeply infiltrated by Christianity. The leaven was working upwards. It was to reach the top (see *The Archaeology of The New Testament* by E. M. Blaiklock, pp. 162–165). Tryphaena and Tryphosa mean 'dainty and delicate'. Paul jokes slyly when he speaks of how they 'laboured to exhaustion' for Christ (such is the force of this verb, 12). Is Rufus, to whom Mark, probably writing in Rome, appears to refer (Mark **15**.21), the brother of Alexander, and son of Simon, who carried the cross? Had they emigrated from Libya (see Acts **11**.20)? And was Nereus the chamberlain of Domitilla, and part of a story of aristocratic Christianity? (Barclay has several pages of reserved conjecture on the list, and the *Expositor's Greek Testament* assembles factual evidence).

> 'They lived not only in ages past,
>   There are hundreds of thousands still,
> The world is bright with the joyous saints
>   Who love to do Jesus' will.
> You can meet them in school, or in lanes, or at sea,
> In church or in trains, or in shops or at tea,
> For the saints of God began just like me,
>   And I mean to be one too.'

Romans 16.17–27   Final Warning

With some abruptness, in the midst of the final salutations, comes a warning. The perennial peril of the Church is faction, and faction so often emerges when some exhibitionist, or aspirant for power, thrusts upon the congregation, in the guise of conviction, and sometimes under the name of God, his own peculiar doctrine (17 f.). Paul had met them in his Galatian churches, at Corinth and Colossae. He feared their intrusion at Philippi (Phil. **3**.18 f.) and at Rome. A man who sets out, in selfish propagation of his own notions, to disturb the peace of the Church, bears a heavy responsibility. As heavy is the burden of guilt upon those who clutter the path to Christ (17). Those who 'by fair and flattering words deceive the hearts of the simple-minded', have been known in all ages. Paul's stern warning is relevant today. He was sure Rome could deal with this intrusion on her unanimity and peace. He hints that such abuses are best nipped in the bud. Perhaps the potential division which has emerged once or twice in this epistle was beginning to crystallize round certain personalities, and Paul may have tactfully thought it wiser to defer the warning to a context remote from his earlier reference to the doctrinal or radical division.

Paul's circle send their greetings. Perhaps they may be identified (see Acts **13**.1; **17**.5–9; **20**.4; 1 Cor. **1**.14; Phil. **2**.19 f.).

Finally, the doxology (25–27). All the leading ideas of the letter may be discovered interwoven in it. This alone is sufficient to defend its authenticity against the doubts which have been raised about its place and authorship.

And so we leave one of the great documents of Christianity and the most difficult of Paul's letters. As with all Scripture which demands hard thinking and searching of the heart, its study is abundantly rewarding.

Questions and subjects for further study and discussion on Romans chs. 14.13—16.27

1. Apply Paul's directions in **14**.22 f. to social situations in which Christians find themselves today.
2. Tolerance should be an active virtue. When passive it could be a vice. Discuss this statement.
3. How does the map reveal the form and scope of Paul's evangelism?
4. Can we expect God always to overrule our mistakes?
5. How could we do more to reproduce the structure of the early Church? The home 'infiltration'?